1 Corinthians

A Devotional of Paul's Letter To Wayward Saints

A Sutliffian Deep Dive Devotional

Paul Sutliff
Introduction by Pastor Luis Diaz

Copyright © 2024 Sutliffian Press

All rights reserved.

No part of this book may be reproduced, stored in a retrieval system, or transmitted by any means, electronic, mechanical, photocopying, recording, or otherwise, without written permission from the author.

ISBN (Paperback): 979-8-9899147-8-4
ISBN (E-book): 979-8-9899147-7-7

Introduction

The historical city of Corinth is in modern-day Greece. A city of prominent stature during the rule of Greece and the rule of Rome, the city found its importance because of its location. Established on an isthmus, which is narrow land dividing two bodies of water, those two bodies are the Corinth Gulf and the Saronic Gulf. Thus, Corinth was a major port city.

In 146 B.C., Rome destroyed the city but later built it back for its strategic purposes. Rome repopulated the city with people from a plurality of backgrounds. It became a major economic and religious metropolis. Only Rome and Alexandria were larger in population. Included, in the population were Jews. This allowed for the spreading of the Gospel.

The book of First Corinthians is a letter penned by the Apostle Paul. Though titled First Corinthians, it is Paul's second letter (5:9). We do not have access to Paul's first letter as it is now lost.

Paul established the church in the city of Corinth on his second missionary journey (Acts 16:9). He spent over a year establishing the church in and around 50-51 A.D. The church immediately developed serious issues upon Paul's departure.

Writing from Ephesus around 54-56 A.D., Paul addressed those issues which included divisions over church leaders, sexual immorality, and lawsuits among believers. In addition, Paul responds to questions posed by the Corinthian church that gave guidance on marriage, foods sacrificed to idols, relationships between men and women, abuses of the Lord's supper, Spiritual gifts, and the resurrection of believers.

Paul finalizes the letter instructing the Corinthians to give a special offering for believers in Jerusalem, final exhortations, and final greetings.

Pastor Luis Diaz

Day #1
I Corinthians 1:1-2

1 Paul, called *to be* an apostle of Jesus Christ through the will of God, and Sosthenes *our* brother,
2 Unto the church of God which is at Corinth, to them that are sanctified in Christ Jesus, called *to be* saints, with all that in every place call upon the name of Jesus Christ our Lord, both theirs and ours:

Paul is writing to the Christians at Corinth. A city known for its pagan worship and sexual immorality. Paul started this church on his second missionary trip and spent about a year and a half there with Aquila and Priscilla doing both evangelism and building the flock up in knowledge and grace.

His opening greeting is very specific. It is not only to the church at Corinth it is to "those that are sanctified in Christ Jesus, called to be saints." This letter is to those who are not playing at being Christians it is to those who believe. Paul not only opens the letter to whom it is addressed to, but he expresses unity with them in whom they serve, the Lord Jesus Christ.

Think about the world we live in today. The world is constantly promoting sex and sexuality in ways that are considered against the Word of God. In a nutshell, the world is pushing and marketing sin to us. This promotion of sinful sexual relations was the norm in Corinth. What it meant to be a Christian there, very much is what it is like to be a Christian here today.

Dear Lord Jesus,

Strengthen me in Your Word. Lord, write Your Word on my heart that I may not sin against You. Help me to stand strong and fast on Your promises. Lord, work on me, change me, make me stronger so that I may stand even if I stand alone so that You may have a witness to the lost.

In Jesus name, Amen.

Day #2
I Corinthians 1:3-9

3   Grace *be* unto you, and peace, from God our Father, and *from* the Lord Jesus Christ.
4   I thank my God always on your behalf, for the grace of God which is given you by Jesus Christ;
5   That in everything you are enriched by him, in all utterance, and *in* all knowledge;
6   Even as the testimony of Christ was confirmed in you:
7   So that you come behind in no gift; waiting for the coming of our Lord Jesus Christ:
8   Who shall also confirm you unto the end, *that you may be* blameless in the day of our Lord Jesus Christ.
9   God *is* faithful, by whom you were called unto the fellowship of his Son Jesus Christ our Lord.

Paul makes it clear in his introduction that the people he is writing to are the believers in Corinth. They are not only confirmed in their belief, they exemplify what it means to follow Christ in that they desire God's will for their lives. Their faith in Christ grows daily. There is nothing, it seems, that holds them back from seeking God.

Ask yourself can this be said about where you worship?

Dear Lord Jesus,

I want to serve you and do better at seeking You first each day. Lord, keep working on me so that I may be stronger and a better example of you to the lost so they may see Your love in how You have changed me.

In Jesus name, Amen.

Day #3
I Corinthians 1:10-17

10   Now I beseech you, brethren, by the name of our Lord Jesus Christ, that you all speak the same thing, and *that* there be no divisions among you; but *that* you be perfectly joined together in the same mind and in the same judgment.

11   For it has been declared unto me of you, my brethren, by them *which are of the house* of Chloe, that there are contentions among you.

12   Now this I say, that every one of you saith, I am of Paul; and I of Apollos; and I of Cephas; and I of Christ.
13   Is Christ divided? Was Paul crucified for you? or were you baptized in the name of Paul?
14   I thank God that I baptized none of you, but Crispus and Gaius;
15   Lest any should say that I had baptized in mine own name.
16   And I baptized also the household of Stephanas: besides, I know not whether I baptized any other.
17   For Christ sent me not to baptize, but to preach the gospel: not with wisdom of words, lest the cross of Christ should be made of none effect.

This section of 1 Corinthians tells us of a problem that is so important members of the church have come to Paul to speak of it. The church is no longer united. It has divisions. The divisions were claimed to be after those who had preached previously. But these were men of God who preached about the Lord Jesus Christ. They did not preach division. So where did these seeds of contention come from? J. Vernon McGee says they came from baby Christians. This is why elders in a church are important. This is why the qualifications to fill those posts are important. Paul was only there a year and a half. Some of the believers there had to mature. Some Christians stay like babies in their faith, never growing. They miss what is important for a small detail that catches their eye that is not important such as who was the evangelist who brought the gospel message.

Paul's message here is that the unity of Christ is important. It overrides the reasons for divisions. This problem of division within the church body is so important that it occupies the first four chapters of this epistle. We as followers of Christ ought to have the mind of Christ and look for what unites us.

Dear Lord Jesus,

Seeking you first is something that should unite all Christians. Lord, I ask that you protect my church family and pastor. Lord let us continue as a united body to express our love of You and You alone. Let us stand and be seen for that Love and unity in You. Lord may we each become such great examples of Your Love that others seek us out to learn of You!

In Jesus name, Amen.

Day #4
I Corinthians 1:18-21

18   For the preaching of the cross is to them that perish foolishness; but unto us which are saved it is the power of God.
19   For it is written, I will destroy the wisdom of the wise, and will bring to nothing the understanding of the prudent.
20   Where *is* the wise? where *is* the scribe? where *is* the disputer of this world? hath not God made foolish the wisdom of this world?
21   For after that in the wisdom of God the world by wisdom knew not God, it pleased God by the foolishness of preaching to save them that believe.

Verse 18 refers to those who perish. Who are they? Those who die without a relationship with Christ. Where do they go? Hell. This preaching of Christ having offered His life freely for the price of the sins of you and I is everything. It is the very power of God, for God to take on this miraculous payment for the burden of payment for our sins. Christ's blood shed on the cross paid that price. There are some with self-proclaimed knowledge that they know better. They may claim that this never happened. Yet it is part of the historical record that Jesus was crucified, that he died and was buried. It is also part of the historical record of the changes wrought in people's lives who believe Jesus died on the cross for them.

Preaching is sharing the Gospel, preaching the truth of Christ's sacrifice for our sins. Preaching is not always done from a pulpit or by a person who is preaching to a crowd. It is done every time a person shares the Good News of Christ with the lost. Preaching is the way people hear of the love of Christ. Are you sharing the love of Christ?

How is the preaching of Christ crucifying the power of God? When God knocks on the door of a person's heart through preaching and he/she accepts that they are indeed a sinner in need of the saving blood of Jesus, the power of God almighty cleanses them from their sins. Is this not a reason to share the GOOD NEWS?

Dear Lord Jesus,

Lord, make me bolder. Lord, may I share Your Word and the gospel message of Your death and resurrection with someone who does not know You. Lord, help me to be Your example to the lost. Help me to be a person who shares Your love in all I do by my words and actions.

In Jesus name, Amen.

Day #5
I Corinthians 1:22-31

22 For the Jews require a sign, and the Greeks seek after wisdom:
23 But we preach Christ crucified, unto the Jews a stumbling block, and unto the Greeks foolishness;
24 But unto them which are called, both Jews and Greeks, Christ the power of God, and the wisdom of God.
25 Because the foolishness of God is wiser than men; and the weakness of God is stronger than men.
26 For you see your calling, brethren, how that not many wise men after the flesh, not many mighty, not many noble, *are called*:
27 But God hath chosen the foolish things of the world to confound the wise; and God has chosen the weak things of the world to confound the things which are mighty;
28 And base things of the world, and things which are despised, has God chosen, *yea*, and things which are not, to bring to nought things that are:
29 That no flesh should glory in his presence.
30 But of him are you in Christ Jesus, who of God is made unto us wisdom, and righteousness, and sanctification, and redemption:
31 That, according as it is written, He that glories, let him glory in the Lord.

"The foolishness of God is wiser than men, and the weakness of God is stronger than men." I have met many men and women who think they know enough to proclaim themselves wise enough to declare there is no God or that there are many ways to heaven. I have been a lover of logic and God's wisdom in creating this knowledge to point out the foolishness of such statements. The more people I meet the more this verse rings true to me. I may never know what the foolishness of God is except that He chose me and the humor in thinking about it is that this choice is wiser than any man. Put yourself in that thought. It should make you smile! Our God loves us so much that His choice for each and every one of us may seem foolish to us, but it is God's wisdom or His foolishness and both are wiser than men! Isn't this a reason to give Him praise and give Him all the glory?

There are so many things in this world that place vanity and love of self above all else. Yet it is the example of Jesus Christ on the cross dying for our sins that teaches us the greatness of self-sacrifice. The greatness of love goes beyond understanding. The greatness of His love that overpowers and envelops us in His arms. There is nothing better. This is a reason to give Him the glory!

Dear Lord Jesus,

I thank You that YOU chose me. I may never understand that as wisdom, but I know Your foolishness is wiser than any human wisdom. Lord, You chose me! You set my feet on Your rock! Mold me and make me after Your will. Move me so that I may stand for You and show others this great unending love that You have to share that breaks down barriers and takes us into your loving arms.

In Jesus name, Amen.

Day #6
I Corinthians 2:1-5

1　And I, brethren, when I came to you, came not with excellency of speech or of wisdom, declaring unto you the testimony of God.
2　For I determined not to know any thing among you, save Jesus Christ, and him crucified.
3　And I was with you in weakness, and in fear, and in much trembling.
4　And my speech and my preaching *was* not with enticing words of man's wisdom, but in demonstration of the Spirit and of power:
5　That your faith should not stand in the wisdom of men, but in the power of God.

Paul preached Jesus Christ crucified dead and buried and risen from the dead. Nothing more and nothing less. The basic simple nature of this message is simply the wisdom of God. No special fancy words can paint the horror and nature of Christ's death in our place. No description of his resurrection with fancy words is needed. This simple message of a man, a chosen weak vessel, by God Almighty was that all God wanted.

Too many today go before men with fancy words and beautiful speech, hoping to do nothing more than earn their keep. When all that is needed is this simple message of Christ crucified, dead, and buried BUT RISEN! You do not need to be a pastor or evangelist to share this message. Paul's message was unrefined. It was raw, it wasn't done with fancy words. He spoke from the heart. He planted seeds. God watered them and many came to a personal relationship with the God who loved them first! You can do this!

Dear Lord Jesus,

    I need Your daring boldness. Lord, use me. Mold me and make me after Your will that I may be one whose life and simple message of You plants seeds of Your love. Lord, may those I know who are bold, and share Christ see the fruit of planting Your seed after You have watered it and it has grown. Lord, may they see the blossoms. May they see the changed lives so that they may be encouraged to never be silent as they go through their daily lives. Lord, may their children also see that fruit and be encouraged to continue in Your Word and Grace that they also may start to share Your Word.

In Jesus name, Amen.

Day #7
I Corinthians 2:6-11

6   Howbeit we speak wisdom among them that are perfect: yet not the wisdom of this world, nor of the princes of this world, that come to nought:

7   But we speak the wisdom of God in a mystery, *even* the hidden *wisdom*, which God ordained before the world unto our glory:

8   Which none of the princes of this world knew: for had they known *it*, they would not have crucified the Lord of glory.
9   But as it is written, Eye hath not seen, nor ear heard, neither have entered into the heart of man, the things which God hath prepared for them that love him.
10   But God hath revealed *them* unto us by his Spirit: for the Spirit searches all things, yea, the deep things of God.
11   For what man knows the things of a man, save the spirit of man which is in him? even so the things of God knows no man, but the Spirit of God.

We are but mortals. We are limited in what we can know and understand. We can't know the future. We may be able to predict it at times. We may be able to guess at things like the weather and use models to predict the behavior of storms and other things. But we can only guess. We cannot know. We, being human are so inferior to God in knowledge. We can barely grasp what we know of God. His very being is so much more than we can understand. This God of love who gives of Himself and demonstrates sacrificial love to us while we are still sinners is something that is hard for us to comprehend. Yet, he gave us the Bible. This God who loves us so desires for us to know of Him and of His love for us. We may not be able to see this knowledge, hear it, or touch it. So, how do we get this knowledge? Can we think of it? No, we have to be granted this knowledge of who Jesus Christ is. Something only God can grant us. Yet we know within us somehow because we are the work of His hands.

Dear Lord Jesus,

Lord, please keep working on me. Please, Lord, help me to know more of You and your love. Lord, help me to see, help me to hear, and much more of who you are. Lord, don't just let me learn more of who You are. Help me to share that knowledge each day.

In Jesus name, Amen.

Day #8
I Corinthians 2:12-16

12   Now we have received, not the spirit of the world, but the spirit which is of God; that we might know the things that are freely given to us of God.

13   Which things also we speak, not in the words which man's wisdom teaches, but which the Holy Ghost teaches; comparing spiritual things with spiritual.

14   But the natural man receives not the things of the Spirit of God: for they are foolishness unto him: neither can he know *them*, because they are spiritually discerned.

15   But he that is spiritual judges all things, yet he himself is judged of no man.

16   For who hath known the mind of the Lord, that he may instruct him? But we have the mind of Christ.

One of the great mysteries of man is how a Christian can read the Bible and see things when a non-believer can read and appear clueless. I admit to seeing this quite a lot with those who like to debate against Christians or read it to claim knowledge. It is somewhat similar to a person with a learning disability not being able to catch inferences from written material. If stated out loud they might catch it. But in written material, it flies over their head. They simply cannot see what others see. A non-believer in the wonder-working power of the blood of Jesus, can read the Bible and totally not get what we see as being common sense understanding from a reading of the Bible. In truth, the Holy Spirit/Ghost reveals these truths to us. It is almost as if a layer of blindness needs to be ripped away in order to grasp what the Bible teaches. This light from the Word of God begins to be seen when a believer seeks to learn more about God from the Bible. The Word of God becomes attached to their hearts, and they begin as believers to lead better lives. They begin to see sin as sin and openly stand on what God has shared with them. Can you see this happening in your life as you read the Bible each day?

Dear Lord Jesus,

You are the God who does impossible things. You continue to work on me and change me through the daily reading of Your Word and my time in prayer. Lord, make Your Word stay in my heart. Help me to meditate on it and share it. Lord, use me I am Yours to use.

In Jesus name, Amen.

Day #9
I Corinthians 3:1-2

1 And I, brethren, could not speak unto you as unto spiritual, but as unto carnal, *even* as unto babes in Christ.
2 I have fed you with milk, and not with meat: for hitherto you were not able *to bear it*, neither yet now are you able.

Here we get to the simple truth that when one comes to Christ, they are believers, but they start as babes in Christ. They are still carnal. They have much to learn before they become spiritual. Paul is not wrong here. Just as we feed babies milk, we must feed babes in Christ the milk of the Word. They need to learn about doctrine, the Bible, and its importance, they need to learn about praying and seeking God. Every one of us is different. Some come to Christ with a fever to learn and a desire to delve into the Word to grow. Others need time to change, and slowly take in the Word of God and the change it creates in them begins to be seen. Carnality is not a statement that they are not Christians. It is a statement that they have not learned much, and there is much that they need to learn.

Dear Lord Jesus,

Help me Lord to grow in You. Strengthen and mold me after Your will. Help me Lord, that I may dig deeper in understanding Your Word. That I may share its simple message and encourage others. Lord, may You be what others see, in me.

In Jesus name, Amen.

Day #10
I Corinthians 3:3-8

3 For you are yet carnal: for whereas *there is* among you envying, and strife, and divisions, are you not carnal, and walk as men?
4 For while one saith, I am of Paul; and another, I *am* of Apollos; are you not carnal?
5 Who then is Paul, and who *is* Apollos, but ministers by whom you believed, even as the Lord gave to every man?
6 I have planted, Apollos watered; but God gave the increase.
7 So then neither is he that plants any thing, neither he that waters; but God that giveth the increase.
8 Now he that plants and he that waters are one: and every man shall receive his own reward according to his own labour.

It seems the Corinthians in their squabbling totally missed the point. Apollos and Paul were not vain men. While it may have appealed to their vanity, to hear people say they follow one or the other, Paul expresses sadness that they seemed to have not grasped that they are not his but Christ's. It seems somewhat silly when we look back at this. Paul expressed the unity of the believers here. He is saying that those who came to Christ came because of God, not because of them. It is God that the people need to credit. Evangelists and preachers/teachers work together to help build up believers in the Word of God. While each of them may like to be credited from time to time for their part, they know that their work is nothing without God doing the work within them.

Dear Lord Jesus,

May You receive the glory for all my work in sharing about You. Let it be known that You and You alone are the reason men's and women's hearts are changed. There is great joy down the road in seeing a babe in Christ become a strong believer. Lord, there is also great joy in seeing that growth blossom. But it is You and You alone who deserve that credit.

In Jesus name, Amen.

Day #11
I Corinthians 3:9-13

9   For we are labourers together with God: you are God's husbandry, *you are* God's building.
10   According to the grace of God which is given unto me, as a wise master-builder, I have laid the foundation, and another builds thereon. But let every man take heed how he builds thereupon.
11   For other foundation can no man lay than that is laid, which is Jesus Christ.
12   Now if any man build upon this foundation gold, silver, precious stones, wood, hay, stubble;

13   Every man's work shall be made manifest: for the day shall declare it, because it shall be revealed by fire; and the fire shall try every man's work of what sort it is.
14   If any man's work abide which he hath built thereupon, he shall receive a reward.
15   If any man's work shall be burned, he shall suffer loss: but he himself shall be saved; yet so as by fire.

Sadly, there are those in the world who seek their own praise and their own vanities. They claim to know Jesus and in truth do not have a relationship with Him. Teachers and preachers like this who "build on" the work of salvation guiding believers towards false doctrines. Their building on the firm foundation of Christ in believers is like wood and stubble. It burns away.

But the metals – when fire touches those it burns away impurities, it gives them a shine. It makes them stand out. Holy fire on something of value to God, what a glossy coat.

Dear Lord Jesus,

Your wondrous holiness resounds as it touches us changing our lives. Some people cannot conceive of a God so powerful and pure that hearts are changed, and lives are transformed not because of what a man does, but because of what God has done for them. Lord, I pray for those small-minded people, that they may learn up close and personal how great and mighty You are, that they would join in the choir singing Your praises.

In Jesus name, Amen.

Day #12
I Corinthians 3:16-17

16 Know you not that you are the temple of God, and *that* the Spirit of God dwelleth in you?
17 If any man defile the temple of God, him shall God destroy; for the temple of God is holy, which *temple* you are.

One of the problems in life is that we as Christians are still sinners. We still do stupid things. We still seek to do that which we know displeases God. Worst of all, as believers, we do this knowingly. Whether this be an act of lust, or any sin imaginable, they are actions that defile the temple of God. We are each a temple of God. We are HIS creation. We are the ones Jesus left the ninety-nine sheep to find the lost one! We are the ones who have been saved by His precious blood offered on the cross as the sacrifice for our sins. Yet, we still do that which we know displeases God. We need to stop living selfishly and living for ourselves. We need to begin to live for HIM and what he did for us. How do we do this? We come before him daily. This means time in prayer, time in reading HIS Word, and time taking those two things into action. God changes us. He does incredible impossible things in us. But we need to give back to Him by living for HIM.

Dear Lord Jesus,

You are the God who does impossible things. Because of that, I know I can come before You and beg that the things that tempt me be made of no effect. Lord, hold me to stand against the fiery darts of the devil through the reading of Your Word. Lord, strengthen me that I might be that light shining on the Hill to show others their way to You.

In Jesus name, Amen.

Day #13
I Corinthians 3:18-23

18 Let no man deceive himself. If any man among you seems to be wise in this world, let him become a fool, that he may be wise.
19 For the wisdom of this world is foolishness with God. For it is written, He takes the wise in their own craftiness.
20 And again, The Lord knows the thoughts of the wise, that they are vain.
21 Therefore let no man glory in men. For all things are yours;
22 Whether Paul, or Apollos, or Cephas, or the world, or life, or death, or things present, or things to come; all are yours;
23 And you are Christ's; and Christ *is* God's.

Vanity is about yourself. Solomon said. "all is vanity." Seeking knowledge to be puffed up is vanity. As Paul says, "the wisdom of this world is foolishness with God." That does not mean it is foolish to seek knowledge. But the seeking of anything, including the attaining of knowledge for the purpose of lifting yourself up is vanity. Even in our thoughts, our vain nature speaks loudly. There, it is all about us. What do we want? What do we desire? Sadly, often the answer to these questions is simple. "Whatever pleases us for the moment." These thoughts are sinful. What does it matter, you may be thinking. But this God who loves us knows our thoughts. For many of us, that should bring shame and fear that this God who loves us so, should be listening to our horribly selfish all about me statements said inside of our heads. But for one thing. God hears our thoughts! He listens to our prayers. We do not need to be loud to be heard by God. We do not need to raise our voices to be heard by the Most High. No, we can be silent, still, and call upon His name and ask of Him what is on our hearts, and HE LISTENS!

Dear Lord Jesus,

You hear my voice whether I speak out loud or silently with the cries of my spirit. You alone hear my silent pleas. You alone answer my simple and often foolish requests. You alone are there for me when there is no one else. Lord, may I be Yours in everything I think, as well as everything I say and do.

In Jesus name, Amen.

Day #14
I Corinthians 4:1

1   Let a man so account of us, as of the ministers of Christ, and stewards of the mysteries of God.

Let us not forget that we all are ministers of Christ. This passage is not about pastors, reverends, and other such persons who work for a church body. It is about each and every believer in the wonder-working power of the blood of Christ. J. Vernon McGee shares that we are all preachers. What are you preaching with your words and actions? If you are an alcoholic what message are sending to the world? If you are a drug addict? A person with no problem engaging in pre-marital sex? A person who has no issues with gossiping? What message are you sending? What are you the steward of? Believers are stewards (keepers) of the mysteries of God.

I find it humorous that God so plainly reveals much of who He is to us, and yet in truth, it shall forever be a mystery that a God can love so far beyond our understanding. Are your words and actions matching up to give a message that you are but one of Jesus Christ's followers washed in HIS blood, cleansed from the stain of your sins? Do your actions and words proclaim that but for God, you would be a miserable person still in your sins on the road to hell?

Dear Lord Jesus,

Help me to change, Lord. Help me to become that precious reflection of the light that shines from Your love. I am but a human, still struggling to do Your will and not my own. I need to become that which You desire over my own thoughts and wants. Lord, keep changing me so I may be a polished gem more perfectly reflecting Your love to others.

In Jesus name, Amen.

Day #15
I Corinthians 4:2-5

2   Moreover it is required in stewards, that a man be found faithful.
3   But with me it is a very small thing that I should be judged of you, or of man's judgment: yea, I judge not mine own self.
4   For I know nothing by myself; yet am I not hereby justified: but he that judges me is the Lord.
5   Therefore judge nothing before the time, until the Lord come, who both will bring to light the hidden things of darkness, and will make manifest the counsels of the hearts: and then shall every man have praise of God.

Stewards must be faithful above all things. They are not required to have many gifts. But they must be faithful. Pastor Alfonso Galvano puts it like this. "They must be consistent." Are you consistent in your walk with Christ? Is it such that it can be seen as consistent by others?

Paul then shares something about the judgement of others. This is the "court of others," which could be seen as undergoing peer influence. What others think about having some effect. But should it? Paul tells us we should not allow that. In this passage that is the lowest court. Then there is the "court of self-judgement." People tend to swing to the ends on this being severe in how the view themselves. They either see all their faults or simply skip over them. Mostly today, people see themselves as high and lofty forgetting their short-comings. But even that court Paul holds in little regard. It is the court of HIS judgement that matters. How does God see us, who knows all that we say, do, and think? That is the place we should trust as honest above our own judgement of ourselves. It is the place deserving of our praise. For even our thoughts and intents are known. No fairer and more revealing judgement can be given.

Dear Lord Jesus,

Help me Lord to see you first in all I say and do. Lord, may your desires become first and foremost in what I think also. These are not easy things to say. I know You, above all others know the true me, above what I know of myself. I am not worthy of your salvation. But somehow, You love even me. Help me Lord, that I may become that faithful steward. Make me stronger and bolder in my faith.

In Jesus name, Amen.

Day #16
I Corinthians 4:6-7

6   And these things, brethren, I have in a figure transferred to myself and *to* Apollos for your sakes; that you might learn in us not to think *of men* above that which is written, that no one of you be puffed up for one against another.

7   For who makes you to differ *from another*? and what have you that you did not receive? now if you did receive *it*, why do you glory, as if you had not received *it*?

These verses can be seen as constructive criticism. Paul points out an error, and why it is an error. Paul is polite. He points out the biggest problem they somehow missed. Paul, Apollos, and others are all simply men. They are not God's Word! On top of that, every one of the Corinthians had simply accepted Christ because of the preaching of one of them. This gift freely given, was received. What grounds if any would vanity have reason to hold? There are none. Paul simply disarmed their vanity. Vanity in general puffs up and makes claims of why this or that is better than something else. But if there is no reason, there is nothing at all to proclaim superiority, vain claims amount to the silliness of a child. Paul's loving nature here is found in these words. "Why do you glory, as if you had not received it?" Paul's proclamation that there is unity in Christ. Unity in being HIS is above all these vain claims stands out.

Dear Lord Jesus,

Lord, help me to stand and not with my own vanity. Lord, may my stand not be on men, but on Your WORD! Lord, help me to proclaim that which is true, right, and just. Help me to also be a person whose actions reflect my words. Lord, help me to lay aside all of my vanity so that YOU alone may be lifted up.

In Jesus name, Amen.

Day #17
I Corinthians 4:8

8   Now you are full, now you are rich, you have reigned as kings without us: and I would to God you did reign, that we also might reign with you.

In verse 8, Paul is on the edge of sarcasm with his wording. Matthew Henry the great Commentator said this:

There is a very elegant gradation from sufficiency to wealth, and thence to royalty, to intimate how much the Corinthians were elated by the abundance of their wisdom and spiritual gifts, which was humor that prevailed among them while the apostle was away from them and made them forget what an interest he had in all. See how apt pride is to over-rate benefits and overlook the benefactor, to swell upon its possessions and forget from whom they come; nay, it is apt to behold them in a magnifying glass: "You have reigned as kings," says the apostle, "that is, in your own conceit; and I would to God you did reign, that we also might reign with you. I wish you had as much of the true glory of a Christian church upon you as you arrogate to yourselves. I should come in then for a share of the honor: I should reign with you: I should not be overlooked by you as now I am, but valued and regarded as a minister of Christ, and a very useful instrument among you." Note, those do not commonly known themselves best who think best of themselves, who have the highest opinion of themselves. The Corinthians might have reigned, and the apostle with them, if they had not been blown up with an imaginary royalty. Note, pride is a great prejudice to our improvement. He is stopped from growing wiser or better, who thinks himself at the height; not only full, but rich, nay, a king.

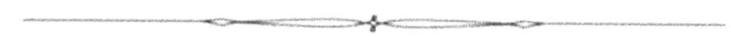

Dear Lord Jesus,

Help me to not forget those who have gone before me. Help me to lift those up who have helped me to grow in Christ. Lord, help me to be a support and encourager to those who help and guide me in Your Word. Lord, help me to honor them by living for You in my words and deeds.

In Jesus name, Amen.

Day #18
I Corinthains 4:9-13

9   For I think that God hath set forth us the apostles last, as it were appointed to death: for we are made a spectacle unto the world, and to angels, and to men.
10 We *are* fools for Christ's sake, but you *are* wise in Christ; we *are* weak, but you *are* strong; you *are* honourable, but we *are* despised.
11 Even unto this present hour we both hunger, and thirst, and are naked, and are buffeted, and have no certain dwelling place;
12 And labour, working with our own hands: being reviled, we bless; being persecuted, we suffer it:
13 Being defamed, we intreat: we are made as the filth of the world, *and are* the offscouring of all things unto this day.

The apostles were men. They were simple in their message. It was united. Jesus died for your sins. He rose from the dead and ascended into heaven. Jesus as God has done all this for you. Yet, that simple message had them attacked. It had them persecuted. The Jews saw this not as a fulfillment of the law but as Jesus making himself God. Thus, they condemned those preaching Christ. They missed the scriptures that hinted that this was God's plan. They skipped over them. So, the simple message given by the apostles was foolishness to them. Paul speaks of how they, the apostles, are treated not to shame them, but to show the difference in treatment. The new Christians in Corinth are considered honorable, or rather they consider themselves honorable. Is this what they should be doing?

Dear Lord Jesus,

Help me to remember those who have served as my spiritual mentors in my prayers to each day. Lord, may I forever remember them and their work. Lord, work on me that I should leave such a legacy of love and action. May my life be an example of Your great love as those who lived that example to me.

In Jesus name, Amen.

Day #19
I Corinthians 4:14-21

14   I write not these things to shame you, but as my beloved sons I warn *you*.
15   For though you have ten thousand instructors in Christ, yet *have you* not many fathers: for in Christ Jesus I have begotten you through the gospel.
16   Wherefore I beseech you, be you followers of me.
17   For this cause have I sent unto you Timotheus, who is my beloved son, and faithful in the Lord, who shall bring you into remembrance of my ways which be in Christ, as I teach every where in every church.
18   Now some are puffed up, as though I would not come to you.

19	But I will come to you shortly, if the Lord will, and will know, not the speech of them which are puffed up, but the power.
20	For the kingdom of God *is* not in word, but in power.
21	What will you? shall I come unto you with a rod, or in love, and *in* the spirit of meekness?

Paul does not demand anything from them. He reminds them that he is their spiritual father and asks only that they remember this and seek to listen to and follow his counsel.

Paul loves the people of the church in Corinth so much that he sends Timothy to them. This act of sending someone to them is an act of caring and concern. Paul does desire to see them again, but God has him doing something else at the time he is writing. He cannot say when he will come but he clearly expresses a desire to be there with them.

Verse 21 is a hint that bigger issues are to come in this letter.

Dear Lord Jesus,

Help me Lord God to stand. Help me that I may not follow men but rather YOU and all that Your Word teaches. Lord, help me to be that example of Your love. Help me to immerse myself in Your wisdom through the reading of Your Word. Use me, Lord. Help me to be the person you want.

In Jesus name, Amen.

Day #20
I Corinthians 5:1

1   It is reported commonly that there is fornication among you, and such fornication as is not so much as named among the Gentiles, that one should have his father's wife.

This report is not gossip. It has been verified. To think that fornication (sex outside of marriage) is known within the church body is bad. But to think that a man would take his father's wife and engage in sexual activity….is horrifically shocking. But to Paul, that is not the worst part. It is that nothing, absolutely nothing has been done by the leaders of the church to show this is not acceptable behavior. Corinth was a mess of sexual permissiveness but even amongst them there were some things that they considered off limits – and this was found in the church. This was not a one-time thing it was an ongoing thing. Something so shocking that its verification was like a billboard that "no sin will be called out here." All is permissible.

There are some who lead churches and never call sin, SIN. They dance around the sins they know that are openly known by those in their church with deep pockets. When Jesus died on the cross for your sins, did he cover the sins of the wealthy more than those who had less? NO! Sin is a slap in God's face it is a choice to disobey HIM. When a member of the church sins openly and is not called for it as opposing that which God calls holy and right, they need to be confronted for the purpose of setting them back on the right path. Restoration is the goal. Can you achieve this if sin is never called sin? NO.

Dear Lord Jesus,

I am a sinner, I come before you begging forgiveness for my sins. Lord, help me to stand up to the tempting things of this world so that I may be that example of Your love and its wonder-working power. Lord, embolden the pastors and leaders in my church to call sin, sin. Lord, strengthen them that they may seek Your guidance to seek restoration of those in need of it. Lord may You strengthen my fellow believers so that they too may stand as examples of Your love. That the church body may be an example of Your great love.

In Jesus name, Amen.

Day #21
I Corinthians 5:2-8

2   And you are puffed up, and have not rather mourned, that he that hath done this deed might be taken away from among you.
3   For I verily, as absent in body, but present in spirit, have judged already, as though I were present, *concerning* him that hath so done this deed,
4   In the name of our Lord Jesus Christ, when you are gathered together, and my spirit, with the power of our Lord Jesus Christ,

5	To deliver such an one unto Satan for the destruction of the flesh, that the spirit may be saved in the day of the Lord Jesus.
6	Your glorying *is* not good. Know you not that a little leaven leaveneth the whole lump?
7	Purge out therefore the old leaven, that you may be a new lump, as you are unleavened. For even Christ our passover is sacrificed for us:
8	Therefore let us keep the feast, not with old leaven, neither with the leaven of malice and wickedness; but with the unleavened *bread* of sincerity and truth.

For restoration to happen sin MUST be called sin! Saying nothing and remaining silent makes the church complicit in that sin. For restoration to occur, they must be separated from the fellowship of believers. They must be set apart as not one of the church as not a believer but a deceiver.

Yes, a deceiver. Because they portrayed themselves as HIS when they would have nothing to do with obeying HIS Word. The church that is silent … it agrees that those sins are normal behavior! That such sin is not sin. It calls GOD a liar!

Please understand, no one wants their sins laid bare for the whole world to see. But in this case, the sinner is so brazen and refuses to change his behavior while insisting he stay as part of the church body. The only alternative left is for the church to oust him. This is not something pleasant. It is not something to rejoice over. But it is good and healthy for the church as the church continues to call sin, sin. It allows the church to stand on God's Word. It allows the church body to be God's representative of His love. What love does not correct and admonish?

Dear Lord Jesus,

Help me Lord to win my own personal struggles against sin. Lord, work on me that I may stand as Your Light to the world so that others may see and understand Your great love. Lord, yes I am a sinner. I am thankful for Your work on the cross. Continue this work in me. Lord, I pray for my church leaders. Lord, make them bold and strong. Enable them to take the strong stands they must so the church may be God's light to the lost.

In Jesus name, Amen.

Day #22
I Corinthians 5:9-13

9 I wrote unto you in an epistle not to company with fornicators:
10 Yet not altogether with the fornicators of this world, or with the covetous, or extortioners, or with idolaters; for then must you needs go out of the world.
11 But now I have written unto you not to keep company, if any man that is called a brother be a fornicator, or covetous, or an idolater, or a railer, or a drunkard, or an extortioner; with such an one no not to eat.
12 For what have I to do to judge them also that are without? do not you judge them that are within?
13 But them that are without God judges. Therefore put away from among yourselves that wicked person.

This passage is about excommunication. It is the putting out of the church, the act of exclusion, and the refusal to allow to associate with the church body. The purpose as stated above is the hope of restoration of that person. Yet there is another purpose, it is that the Bride of Christ, the church, may be seen as living as an example of HIS love.

Verse 11 has been used out of context to tell some not to associate with sinners, not to ever sit down to a meal with them, and more. That sounds like excluding those who need Jesus from learning about Him. Instead, this passage is about the exclusion of those within the church body who are engaging in such sins that make him/her out to mock Christ by how they live. We must be examples of how Christ has changed our lives. We must live lives dedicated to Him and His love for us. How can this be seen, when such sin abounds openly in a church body?

Dear Lord Jesus,

Your love changed me. Lord, help me to share that love. Lord, help me to point others to this wondrous change that you have done in my life. Lord, may I be that beacon on a hill that shines a light on You. Lord, please continue to work on me. I know I have a ways to go.

In Jesus name, Amen.

Day #23
I Corinthians 6:1-10

1. Dare any of you, having a matter against another, go to law before the unjust, and not before the saints?
2. Do you not know that the saints shall judge the world? And if the world shall be judged by you, are you unworthy to judge the smallest matters?
3. Know you not that we shall judge angels? How much more things that pertain to this life?
4. If then you have judgments of things pertaining to this life, set them to judge who are least esteemed in the church.
5. I speak to your shame. Is it so, that there is not a wise man among you? No, not one that shall be able to judge between his brethren?
6. But brother goes to law with brother, and that before the unbelievers.
7. Now therefore there is utterly a fault among you, because you go to law one with another. Why do you not rather take wrong? Why do you not rather *allow yourselves to* be defrauded?
8. Nay, you do wrong, and defraud, and that *your* brethren.
9. Know you not that the unrighteous shall not inherit the kingdom of God? Be not deceived: neither fornicators, nor idolaters, nor adulterers, nor effeminate, nor abusers of themselves with mankind,
10. Nor thieves, nor covetous, nor drunkards, nor revilers, nor extortioners, shall inherit the kingdom of God.

In verse 1, Paul is not saying that you should not go to court, but rather that matters between believers should be dealt with within the church. There are several reasons for this. The foremost being that secular authorities are not equipped to address anything outside of the law. The spiritual matters that should unite us, as believers should reign supreme over our ability to be divided and having issues with one another. Is Paul suggesting churches should have a separate court system to deal only with Christians? No. Rather he is suggesting that we do all in our power to not bring things to a court and rather seek a resolution between the parties that satisfies both. Why should such a matter be bared to the public and show division rather than unity in Christ?

Paul restates in verses 9 and 10, the sins that distinguish those who state they believe from those who have not faith. Some sins do distinguish people from others as not belonging in a position of leadership, especially in a Christian setting, for these sins are open declarations of a lack of belief and devotion to Christ.

Now think of the secular authorities as having such sinfulness in their authorities over those of the believers. Can such truly be trusted to give a wise and moral judgement?

Dear Lord Jesus,

Help me in my unbelief to be molded to your desires Lord. Work on me that I should be an example of Your love. Lord, remind me to communicate with my fellow believers when something happens that bothers me. Lord, may I both easily forgive and easily dismiss both the small things and things that appear big to me. For Lord, I know the unity of believers is more important than anything I think is important.

In Jesus name, Amen.

Day #24
I Corinthians 6:9-11

9   Know you not that the unrighteous shall not inherit the kingdom of God? Be not deceived: neither fornicators, nor idolaters, nor adulterers, nor effeminate, nor abusers of themselves with mankind,
10   Nor thieves, nor covetous, nor drunkards, nor revilers, nor extortioners, shall inherit the kingdom of God.
11   And such were some of you: but you are washed, but you are sanctified, but you are justified in the name of the Lord Jesus, and by the Spirit of our God.

In verses 9 and 10, there is a list of sins, some of those listed are also known as crimes. When a person comes to Christ, he/should have lost those things behind as recognition that these were things God was not pleased with in their lives. These were the sinful things that brought them to the cross to seek forgiveness. The thought of these behaviors continuing inside the church is not acceptable. It goes against all that Christ taught us. How can the believer be the one to inherit the kingdom of God when they also commit these sins? These are the things that are supposed to be left behind in your old life. These are the things you walked away from. In the church, it matters not what you came from but who You are living for! Are you not washed in His blood? Are you not sanctified and justified because of the work of Christ? These things ought not to be in the church body.

Dear Lord Jesus,

You have washed me and sanctified me in your shed blood. Lord, I owe you everything that I am. Lord, may my life shine in the difference that You have made in my life. Lord, please continue to work on me so that I may be that beacon the hill pointing the way to You so others may find Your great forgiving all-encompassing love.

In Jesus name, Amen.

Day #25
I Corinthians 6:12-20

12 All things are lawful unto me, but all things are not expedient: all things are lawful for me, but I will not be brought under the power of any.
13 Meats for the belly, and the belly for meats: but God shall destroy both it and them. Now the body *is* not for fornication, but for the Lord; and the Lord for the body.
14 And God hath both raised up the Lord, and will also raise up us by his own power.
15 Know you not that your bodies are the members of Christ? shall I then take the members of Christ, and make *them* the members of an harlot? God forbid.
16 What? know you not that he which is joined to an harlot is one body? for two, saith he, shall be one flesh.
17 But he that is joined unto the Lord is one spirit.

18   Flee fornication. Every sin that a man doeth is without the body; but he that commits fornication sins against his own body.
19   What? know you not that your body is the temple of the Holy Ghost *which is* in you, which you have of God, and you are not your own?
20   For you are bought with a price: therefore glorify God in your body, and in your spirit, which are God's.

Just because something is legal to do does not mean you should engage in that activity. Fornication may or may not be legal where you live, but that does not mean it is something acceptable to God. It is a sin with many ramifications. The sin is not only against God, it is against your own body as much as putting poison in your body. This can be seen as simply as looking at the spread of sexually transmitted diseases. These things cannot enter your body if you do not engage in such sins AND if your intention has also entered the marriage pure. Think about what this means regarding our thoughts on this matter.

Dear Lord Jesus,

Help me Lord to keep myself pure in body for You. Lord, may I stand on Your Word. May I be that example of Your love. Lord, you bought me with a price. Help me to honor that price which You paid with my devotion to follow Your will.

In Jesus name, Amen.

Day #26
I Corinthians 7:1-2

1   Now concerning the things whereof you wrote unto me: *it is* good for a man not to touch a woman.
2   Nevertheless, *to avoid* fornication, let every man have his own wife, and let every woman have her own husband.

This passage is a simple recognition that there are natural sinful desires within men and women that are by themselves not sinful within the context of marriage. Sexual relations within marriage are not sinful. This is important to understand because some teach that acts of sexual relation are by themselves sins even in a marriage. Paul is sharing here that such a belief is not only wrong but that the actions of sexual relations within marriage are not sinful but acceptable to God.

Paul also shares here an equality between males and females in marriage. The having of each other. Yes, the man is to be the leader, but in marriage, there is equality that is good.

Dear Lord Jesus,

I praise you for sharing with us this simple truth that many distort. Lord, I pray that there would be more displays of honoring marriage vows. Lord, may we as men and women who love You and honor You lift up marriage. May the Church become such a beacon of what marriage is and should be, that the world seeks out the church and finds Your love as a result.

In Jesus name, Amen.

Day #27
I Corinthians 7:3-7

3   Let the husband render unto the wife due benevolence: and likewise also the wife unto the husband.
4   The wife hath not power of her own body, but the husband: and likewise also the husband has not power of his own body, but the wife.
5   Defraud you not one the other, except *it be* with consent for a time, that you may give yourselves to fasting and prayer; and come together again, that Satan tempt you not for your incontinency.
6   But I speak this by permission, *and* not of commandment.
7   For I would that all men were even as I myself. But every man hath his proper gift of God, one after this manner, and another after that.

Paul describes the women in a marriage here as gifts from God to their husbands. When you receive a gift, it has a special meaning. You should love and cherish it. He encourages both husbands and wives to enjoy their sexual relations inside the marriage, not denying the desires of the other, except during a time of fasting when both agree.

Marriage is a gift from God, Paul says here. It is not a commandment. It is something to be encouraged. Without it, there are no permissible sexual relations.

Dear Lord Jesus,

Please strengthen the marriages of those in my church. Lord, may those who are married renew their vows in their hearts and minds with a commitment to honor You.

In Jesus name, Amen.

Day #28
I Corinthians 7:8-9

8   I say therefore to the unmarried and widows, It is good for them if they abide even as I.

9   But if they cannot contain, let them marry: for it is better to marry than to burn.

Paul recognized that living a single life if unmarried was best. There are advantages to being single. You do not have someone else to take care of, nor do you have someone thinking just of you. Paul recognized that this might be well and good, but there are desires and temptations that can be put to rest through marriage. These verses address those who choose to "live together" without also getting married. They are living a life that may be "committed" to each other without endorsing it with God's will for them, which is marriage. Without marriage, there is no declared open statement of belonging to each other. There is nothing that states on paper, or in action that two are willing to be there for each other through both the good and bad times. Today, many engage in living together, rather than entering into marriage. They choose not to allow God's blessing on their bond to one another. They refuse to allow the blessing God has for them and instead accumulate sin.

Dear Lord Jesus,

May Your overpowering love reach those who choose to live together avoiding the bond of marriage. Lord, may You break down the walls they put up to avoid marrying. Lord, help them to see that marriage is Your desire and that it comes with Your blessings.

In Jesus name, Amen.

Day #29
I Corinthians 7:10-17

10   And unto the married I command, *yet* not I, but the Lord, Let not the wife depart from *her* husband:
11   But and if she depart, let her remain unmarried, or be reconciled to *her* husband: and let not the husband put away *his* wife.

12   But to the rest speak I, not the Lord: If any brother hath a wife that believeth not, and she be pleased to dwell with him, let him not put her away.
13   And the woman which hath an husband that believeth not, and if he be pleased to dwell with her, let her not leave him.
14   For the unbelieving husband is sanctified by the wife, and the unbelieving wife is sanctified by the husband: else were your children unclean; but now are they holy.
15   But if the unbelieving depart, let him depart. A brother or a sister is not under bondage in such *cases*: but God hath called us to peace.
16   For what know you, O wife, whether you shalt save your husband? or how know you, O man, whether you shalt save your wife?
17   But as God hath distributed to every man, as the Lord hath called every one, so let him walk. And so ordain I in all churches.

Basically, this passage says "divorce is a dirty word." Being unequally yoked, and being married to one who is not a Christian is not grounds for a divorce. This is important. There are many cults out there that insist that when a spouse leaves their fold, a divorce happens. Christianity centers on God's love for man. We are to live such a life that we become examples of that love. Leaving a spouse is not an example of love. There are legitimate reasons to leave a marriage, such as abuse.

Dear Lord Jesus,

    Help me Lord in my unbelief to stand strong as an example of Your great love. Lord, be my strength and shelter to help me to keep my commitments when I am weak. Lord, work on me, make me stronger as an example of Your love that others may see You.

In Jesus name, Amen.

Day #30
I Corinthians 7:18-24

18   Is any man called being circumcised? let him not become uncircumcised. Is any called in uncircumcision? let him not be circumcised.
19   Circumcision is nothing, and uncircumcision is nothing, but the keeping of the commandments of God.
20   Let every man abide in the same calling wherein he was called.
21   Are you called *being* a servant? care not for it: but if you may be made free, use *it* rather.
22   For he that is called in the Lord, *being* a servant, is the Lord's freeman: likewise also he that is called, *being* free, is Christ's servant.
23   You are bought with a price; be not you the servants of men.
24   Brethren, let every man, wherein he is called, there in abide with God.

You are bought with a price. Yes, you! Our entire salvation is based on the price that was paid by Jesus Christ on the cross for our sins. Why should we allow things to separate us? Circumcision is nothing. Our positions in life are nothing. We as believers should unite and stand together as one. After all, this price that was paid was not paid by you or me. It was paid by Christ. We should see this as something that unites us above all else.

There are beliefs that are essential to being a Christian. These are called essential doctrines. They set us apart from others and unify us. Then there are other doctrines. These small differences really don't matter. We are one! This is Paul's message to the Corinthians to think more about what unites us than that which divides us.

Dear Lord Jesus,

Lord, help me to see the things that unite us as believers above the things that divide us. Help me to be someone who lifts up and encourages my brother and sister in Christ. Help me to be someone who unifies the body of Christ in word and deed. Lord, please keep working on me so that I may be someone whose life points to the greatness of Your work on the cross through my words and deeds.

In Jesus name, Amen.

Day #31
I Corinthians 7:25-26

25   Now concerning virgins I have no commandment of the Lord: yet I give my judgment, as one that hath obtained mercy of the Lord to be faithful.
26   I suppose therefore that this is good for the present distress, *I say*, that *it is* good for a man so to be.

Here Paul tells the Corinthians the Lord does not have commandments for everything. Some things are up to you and your relationship with God. Paul states in his position as an Apostle, that he thinks it is good to remain a virgin. It is quite specific. It means remaining sexually pure. It does not mean staying single and jumping from bed to bed. There are commandments on remaining sexually pure both in and out of marriage. There is no commandment saying not to marry. Paul is not speaking to just those who are single. He is speaking only to those who have not engaged in sexual activity. The past religion of the area had parents bringing their virgin sons and daughters to gods like Aphrodite to be engaged in service. Paul is saying there is no need to rush marrying. It is okay and good to remain a virgin. It is to be encouraged to be sexually pure.

Dear Lord Jesus,

Lord, I pray for those who are virgins, Lord that You would strengthen to wait until they marry the man/woman you have for them. Lord, strengthen their resolve. Help them to grow in You and understand that Your timing is best.

In Jesus name, Amen.

Day #32
I Corinthians 7:27-28

27 Are you bound unto a wife? seek not to be loosed. Are you loosed from a wife? seek not a wife.
28 But and if you marry, you have not sinned; and if a virgin marry, she has not sinned. Nevertheless such shall have trouble in the flesh: but I spare you.

These two verses are important to those who believe and have divorced. There are some who teach that a divorced person for whatever reason is not allowed to marry again. But here it is very plain and openly stated that it is not a sin to do so, but there will be trouble in the flesh. Anyone who has divorced understands marriage has its troubles and its joys. The idea of marrying again means a person brings baggage from their previous marriage into the new marriage. Paul's advise here is important. It is good not to seek to remarry, but to do so is not a sin.

Dear Lord Jesus,

Your Word gives answers before we know we would need such answers. Lord, help me to live a life dedicated to You. Lord, mold me and make me stronger in my faith and stronger in my example and my ability to point to You so that others may see You.

In Jesus name, Amen.

Day #33
I Corinthians 7:29-31

29   But this I say, brethren, the time *is* short: it remains, that both they that have wives be as though they had none;
30   And they that weep, as though they wept not; and they that rejoice, as though they rejoiced not; and they that buy, as though they possessed not;
31   And they that use this world, as not abusing *it*: for the fashion of this world passes away.

The great commentator Matthew Henry saw these verses as guides/rules that Christians should follow. What would Christians around the world be like if all of us took this advice? Here are the rules Matthew Henry saw in these verses:

1. As to relations: Those that had wives must be as though they had none; that is, they must not set their hearts too much on the comforts of the relation; they must be as though they had

none. They know not how soon they shall have none. This advice must be carried into every other relation. Those who have children should be as though they had none. Those that are their comfort now may prove their greatest cross. And soon may the flower of all comforts be cut down.

2. As to afflictions: Those that weep must be as though they wept not; that is, we must not be dejected too much with any of our afflictions, nor indulge ourselves in the sorrow of the world, but keep up a holy joy in God in the midst of all our troubles, so that even in sorrow the heart may be joyful, and the end of our grief may be gladness. Weeping may endure for a night, but joy will come in the morning. If we can but get to heaven at last, all tears shall be wiped from our eyes; and the prospect of it now should make us moderate our sorrows and refrain our tears.

3. As to worldly enjoyments: Those that rejoice should be as though they rejoiced not; that is, they should not take too great a complacency in any of their comforts. They must be moderate in their mirth and sit loose to the enjoyments they most value. Here is not their rest, nor are these things their portion; and therefore, their hearts should not be set on them, nor should they place their solace or satisfaction in them.

4. As to worldly traffic and employment: Those that buy must be as though they possessed not. Those who prosper in trade, increase in wealth, and purchase estates, should hold these possessions as though they held them not. It is but setting their hearts on that which is not (Prov. 23:5) to do otherwise. Buying and possessing should not too much engage our minds. They hinder many people altogether from minding the better part. Purchasing land and trying oxen kept the guests invited from the wedding supper, Lu. 14:18, 19. And, when they do not altogether hinder men from minding their

chief business, they do very much divert them from a close pursuit. Those are most likely to run so as to obtain the prize who ease their minds of all foreign cares and cumbrances.

5. As to all worldly concerns: Those that use this world as not abusing it, v. 31. The world may be used, but must not be abused. It is abused when it is not used to those purposes for which it is given, to honor God and do good to men when, instead of being oil to the wheels of our obedience, it is made fuel to lust-when, instead of being a servant, it is made our master, our idol, and has that room in our affections which should be reserved for God. And there is great danger of abusing it in all these respects if our hearts are too much set upon it. We must keep the world as much as may be out of our hearts, that we may not abuse it when we have it in our hands.

Dear Lord Jesus,

Help me Lord to more closely follow Your Word. Lord, put Your Word in my heart so that I may not only learn Your Word but that I may more easily live it. Lord, please continue to work on me so that my life may point to Your great love as that which we cannot do without.

In Jesus name, Amen.

Day #34
I Corinthians 7:32-35

32   But I would have you without carefulness. He that is unmarried cares for the things that belong to the Lord, how he may please the Lord:
33   But he that is married cares for the things that are of the world, how he may please *his* wife.
34   There is difference *also* between a wife and a virgin. The unmarried woman cares for the things of the Lord, that she may be holy both in body and in spirit: but she that is married cares for the things of the world, how she may please *her* husband.
35   And this I speak for your own profit; not that I may cast a snare upon you, but for that which is comely, and that you may attend upon the Lord without distraction.

Paul here shares about the differences between those that are married and those that are not, in serving the Lord. Those who are married have more care than that of themselves and the Lord. The wife thinks of herself, her children if she has any, and of the world's ability to help her make her husband happy. The husband also in thinking of the wife, thinks of things in the world that would make her happy or himself happy. He also thinks of the children before himself. I know children are not mentioned in this passage, but this is part and parcel of marriage.

Paul's point here is that marriage can be a distraction when you are serving the Lord and that remaining single is preferable.

Anyone married can share how their thoughts are constantly of their spouse and children. This is not a bad thing. But the unmarried one has more time to devote to the things of God.

Dear Lord Jesus,

May You bless those who are married as Christians. May You also bless those who are unmarried to keep that focus on You. Lord, there is nothing under the sun that is new to You. Lord, please continue to mold me and make me into that special someone who points straight to You so that others may find Your love.

In Jesus name, Amen.

Day #35
I Corinthians 7:36-40

36   But if any man think that he behaves himself uncomely toward his virgin, if she pass the flower of *her* age, and need so require, let him do what he will, he sins not: let them marry.

37   Nevertheless he that stands steadfast in his heart, having no necessity, but hath power over his own will, and hath so decreed in his heart that he will keep his virgin, doeth well.

38   So then he that giveth *her* in marriage doeth well; but he that giveth *her* not in marriage doeth better.

39 The wife is bound by the law as long as her husband lives; but if her husband be dead, she is at liberty to be married to whom she will; only in the Lord.
40 But she is happier if she so abide, after my judgment: and I think also that I have the Spirit of God.

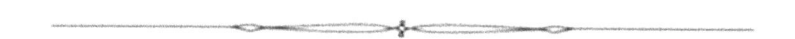

Paul has said that it is up to the individual to choose whether or not to be married. He has also put the choice on the parent. Culture has an allowance for marriage arrangements by parents, so Paul also puts that choice on the parents. Paul also includes here the choice of the widow to remarry after her husband has passed away. She may remarry. It is her choice. Paul has said these things are his personal judgement, not God's. Yet he does not want us to forget who he is as God's servant.

Dear Lord Jesus,

May You finish the work you have begun in me. Lord, I beg of You, that you continue to change me and mold me into that person people can see as someone who loves You. Lord may I be that light shining the way to the true LIGHT, YOU.

In Jesus name, Amen.

Day #36
I Corinthians 8:1-4

1   Now as touching things offered unto idols, we know that we all have knowledge. Knowledge puffs up, but charity edifies.
2   And if any man think that he knows any thing, he knows nothing yet as he ought to know.
3   But if any man love God, the same is known of him.
4   As concerning therefore the eating of those things that are offered in sacrifice unto idols, we know that an idol *is* nothing in the world, and that *there is* none other God but one.

It is funny how when we learn something, nothing new it can excite us and make us feel great. Yet, there are some who do not see how that first little bit of knowledge is the tip of the iceberg of knowledge in that area. They think they know it all. That bit of knowledge has them acting like a peacock strutting around as if they know everything to know on that one issue, when they know so little about it, that they appear as a fool. Part of being a Christian is admitting when we do not know things and being willing to learn what we do not know about some things. Paul clarifies something important here in verses 2 and 3. Knowledge puffs us up, but love BUILDS UP!

This passage referred to the eating of meat offered to idols. It would be the choicest meat. The best was given to their gods. It is not clear in this passage if Christians were simply taking the meat offering to idols after it was placed, or if they are buying it at a market. Yes, Christians know there are no other gods than the one true and living God.

Dear Lord Jesus,

Help me Lord to recognize my smallness in what I do know. You know all things, what am I, compared to Your great and vast knowledge. Lord, please direct me to the things You wish me to learn more of. Help me to see those things which are good and right and of You first and foremost. Lord, You alone have set me on Your path. Lord, work on me that I may grow in the knowledge of You above all else.

In Jesus name, Amen.

Day #37
I Corinthians 8:5-13

5   For though there be that are called gods, whether in heaven or in earth, (as there be gods many, and lords many,)
6   But to us *there is but* one God, the Father, of whom *are* all things, and we in him; and one Lord Jesus Christ, by whom *are* all things, and we by him.
7   Howbeit *there is* not in every man that knowledge: for some with conscience of the idol unto this hour eat *it* as a thing offered unto an idol; and their conscience being weak is defiled.

8	But meat commends us not to God: for neither, if we eat, are we the better; neither, if we eat not, are we the worse.
9	But take heed lest by any means this liberty of yours become a stumbling block to them that are weak.
10	For if any man see you which hast knowledge sit at meat in the idol's temple, shall not the conscience of him which is weak be emboldened to eat those things which are offered to idols;
11	And through your knowledge shall the weak brother perish, for whom Christ died?
12	But when you sin so against the brethren, and wound their weak conscience, you sin against Christ.
13	Wherefore, if meat make my brother to offend, I will eat no flesh while the world stands, lest I make my brother to offend.

Sometimes doing something that is not a sin can be thought of as bad by those who are young in the Lord. These are the new babes in Christ or the ones who do not choose to grow. We do not want to create stumbling blocks for them. Rather we want to be encouraged in their growth. In the time Paul wrote this letter taking meat offered to idols, which were for false gods was not a sin, since these are fake and false gods. It was the best meat. Which indeed means it was tempting. No matter how this best meat was obtained from the idols, some saw this as problematic. Paul saw this issue and said we should do nothing to offend a fellow believer.

During the time of COVID, this has meant wearing a mask and social distancing for those with little faith at one point. That moved to letting them wear masks without questioning them about living in fear. We as Christ's loved ones must live for HIM. That means accepting that the young in Christ have much to learn and doing what we can to encourage them in the faith.

Dear Lord Jesus,

You have been patient with me. You have corrected me. You have set me back on the right path time and time again. Lord, help me to be as You are towards others whose faith has not yet grown. Lord, help me to be one who is able to point to You.

In Jesus name, Amen.

Day #38
I Corinthians 9:1-2

1   Am I not an apostle? am I not free? have I not seen Jesus Christ our Lord? are not you my work in the Lord?
2   If I be not an apostle unto others, yet doubtless I am to you: for the seal of mine apostleship are you in the Lord.

Paul here is exerting his title of Apostle. Apostle means, "sent out from the Lord." Paul was commissioned by the Christ after His resurrection. An apostle is not unlike a missionary. The fruit of a missionary's work is the salvation of those who hear the Word of God and the changing of lives as they grow in Christ. For an apostle and a missionary, those who changed lives, those who gave their lives to Christ are a testimony to the truth and reality of the work of Christ on the cross. But they are also a seal of the authority of the apostle and the missionary. They are a testimony to their work for Christ.

We have been given the Great Commission to preach Christ crucified, dead and buried, and risen on the third day. We are to share the wonder working power of Christ's sacrifice for our sins and the incredible miracle of Christ's resurrection. We may not be apostles, but we are included in the Great Commission. Who have we shared Christ with? Who have we stepped out of our comfort zone to share the things Christ has done in our lives?

Dear Lord Jesus,

I need your boldness. I need your strength to stop being silent and become a real friend to those I know by sharing the work You have done in me. Lord, I would not be here without the incredible work You have done in my life. Lord, help me to share this love You had, for even me. Help me to get out of my comfort zone and share with others who You are and what You have done in my life.

In Jesus name, Amen.

Day #39
I Corinthians 9:3-11

3 Mine answer to them that do examine me is this,
4 Have we not power to eat and to drink?
5 Have we not power to lead about a sister, a wife, as well as other apostles, and *as* the brethren of the Lord, and Cephas?
6 Or I only and Barnabas, have not we power to forbear working?
7 Who goes a warfare any time at his own charges? who plants a vineyard, and eats not of the fruit thereof? or who feeds a flock, and eats not of the milk of the flock?
8 Say I these things as a man? or saith not the law the same also?
9 For it is written in the law of Moses, You shalt not muzzle the mouth of the ox that treads out the corn. Doth God take care for oxen?
10 Or saith he *it* altogether for our sakes? For our sakes, no doubt, *this* is written: that he that plows should plow in hope; and that he that threshes in hope should be partaker of his hope.
11 If we have sown unto you spiritual things, *is it* a great thing if we shall reap your carnal things?

In verses 1 and 2, Paul talked about his authority as an apostle. In verses 3 to 6, he expresses that apostles are human. They eat and drink, some support wives and family. Some have jobs they hold in order to support themselves and their family. In verses 7 to 11, we have Paul tackling the topic of why a pastor/preacher/missionary should be paid.

Paul gives a powerful argument in that the Word of God orders them not to muzzle the ox as it treads out the corn. This says something about how we treat those who do provide us with spiritual gifts. If we benefit, should we not be rewarding them? If we are to reward an ox for his work, how much more so the preacher/pastor/evangelist, etc.? The sad truth is that there are some who think that pastors, preachers, evangelists, etc. should be working for free. They ignore that they are human and need to eat and also provide for their families. Some are stingy in what they give to support the person who provides spiritual benefits for them. Paul is not asking someone to support those who is struggling financially to support themselves. Paul is simply communicating that there is a need to support the person/s that provide you with the spiritual blessing you receive.

Dear Lord Jesus,

Help me to bless my pastor(s) through my tithes and offerings. Lord, may You continue to watch over them and their families. Lord, send angels to protect these great servants of Yours. Lord, please keep them on the right track. They deserve so much more than I am capable of blessing them with. Lord, please do not let me forget how much they have helped me to grow.

In Jesus name, Amen.

Day #40
I Corinthians 9:12-16

12   If others be partakers of *this* power over you, *are* not we rather? Nevertheless we have not used this power; but suffer all things, lest we should hinder the gospel of Christ.
13   Do you not know that they which minister about holy things live *of the things* of the temple? and they which wait at the altar are partakers with the altar?
14   Even so hath the Lord ordained that they which preach the gospel should live of the gospel.
15   But I have used none of these things: neither have I written these things, that it should be so done unto me: for *it were* better for me to die, than that any man should make my glorying void.
16   For though I preach the gospel, I have nothing to glory of: for necessity is laid upon me; yea, woe is unto me, if I preach not the gospel!

Paul continues on the theme of paying the preacher here, but Paul has been a tent maker. He preaches the Gospel of Christ, and expecting no gifts, he works for his pay making tents. Paul didn't take income from those he preached and taught. Yet, he did not preach about paying the person who ministers unto them that he should start to be paid. He instead laid out the facts from the scripture that truth may be told as he based his ministry on. The truth of the power of the wondering working power of Christ shed blood on the cross was all too important to not share. Its importance compelled him to share the Gospel. He felt this passion about sharing Jesus so much that he could not be silent. Is that not how we should be about sharing Christ?

Dear Lord Jesus,

Work on me. Change me and give me boldness that I may share Your wonder-working power in the changing of my life and that power to change others' lives. Lord, use me that I may share Your greatness. Use me that I may be one though small and slight as a beacon that points and directs others to Your powerful wonder-working love.

In Jesus name, Amen.

Day #41
I Corinthians 9:17-27

17   For if I do this thing willingly, I have a reward: but if against my will, a dispensation *of the gospel* is committed unto me.
18   What is my reward then? *Verily* that, when I preach the gospel, I may make the gospel of Christ without charge, that I abuse not my power in the gospel.
19   For though I be free from all *men*, yet have I made myself servant unto all, that I might gain the more.
20   And unto the Jews I became as a Jew, that I might gain the Jews; to them that are under the law, as under the law, that I might gain them that are under the law;

21 To them that are without law, as without law, (being not without law to God, but under the law to Christ,) that I might gain them that are without law.

22 To the weak became I as weak, that I might gain the weak: I am made all things to all *men*, that I might by all means save some.

23 And this I do for the gospel's sake, that I might be partaker thereof with *you*.

24 Know you not that they which run in a race run all, but one receives the prize? So run, that you may obtain.

25 And every man that strives for the mastery is temperate in all things. Now they *do it* to obtain a corruptible crown; but we an incorruptible.

26 I therefore so run, not as uncertainly; so fight I, not as one that beats the air:

27 But I keep under my body, and bring *it* into subjection: lest that by any means, when I have preached to others, I myself should be a castaway.

Paul has said preachers should be paid. Yet he did not take payment and worked as a tent maker for income. So why does he share the Gospel? What can he get out of doing this? Paul shares that he is in a race. A race is urgent, the time is limited. There is an end and a finish line. The rewards are beyond our understanding, and they are heavenly. What a race it is indeed!

We know that Jesus is coming back and we do not know when this will happen. It could happen tomorrow or the next hour. What are you and I doing to share the Gospel today? We need to be in that race! We need to think like we do when we pursue knowledge to raise our understanding of whether to master a skill or to become an expert in a field. We need to become the best we can be at sharing the Gospel. This is something we as believers should be engaging in. When was the last time you pursued the incorruptible crown Paul speaks of? What have you done to increase your knowledge in sharing Christ with others?

Live your life for Christ, putting your body into subjection to HIS will, and join the race!

Dear Lord Jesus,

I am nothing but You, You are everything! Lord use me. Embolden me and place me where I can share Your Word. Use me so that I may encourage others to find Your great redeeming Love. Help me to join in this race for that incorruptible crown. Lord, I want to share You. Help me to do this.

In Jesus name, Amen.

Day #42
I Corinthians 10:1-5

1	Moreover, brethren, I would not that you should be ignorant, how that all our fathers were under the cloud, and all passed through the sea;
2	And were all baptized unto Moses in the cloud and in the sea;
3	And did all eat the same spiritual meat;

4   And did all drink the same spiritual drink: for they drank of that spiritual Rock that followed them: and that Rock was Christ.
5   But with many of them God was not well pleased: for they were overthrown in the wilderness.

The church of Corinth was comprised of both Jews and Gentiles. Paul went first to the Jews. The fathers here are the ancestors of the Jews. These ancestors were at the edge of the Red Sea. They saw Pharaoh's army coming and began to complain to Moses that they should go back to Egypt, go back to the slavery God had freed them from! They had little to no faith. Yet God appears through a fiery pillar of cloud and protects them. Yet, they do not see a reason for faith. Moses followed God's direction and stretched out his hands over the sea and the sea parted. A whole night passed when a wind blew over that parted sea then they walked on dry ground into the parted sea. They pass through the sea because of the faith of Moses, not because of their own faith in God. They sing a victory song of Moses after they pass over and the Egyptian army is vanquished by God. They feel free without the fear of being brought back for the first time. They did everything they were supposed to do because of the faith of Moses.

They complained, they rebelled. Yet because of the faith of Moses, they had been redeemed. Christian liberty is like this. We have salvation through the work of Christ. Yet we still need to make choices to follow HIM rather than our own desires and lusts. There are choices left to you. Which direction will you choose?

Dear Lord Jesus,

I know it is not in me to direct my own footsteps. Lord, be my guide. Put my feet on the way which is right. Help me to set my heart, mind, and body in the way that You choose for me. Lead me. Help me to put aside those things which distract me from doing that which You desire for me to do. Lord, please use me. I am Yours.

In Jesus name, Amen.

Day #43
I Corinthians 10:6-10

6	Now these things were our examples, to the intent we should not lust after evil things, as they also lusted.
7	Neither be you idolaters, as *were* some of them; as it is written, The people sat down to eat and drink, and rose up to play.
8	Neither let us commit fornication, as some of them committed, and fell in one day three and twenty thousand.
9	Neither let us tempt Christ, as some of them also tempted, and were destroyed of serpents.
10	Neither murmur you, as some of them also murmured, and were destroyed of the destroyer.

The children of Israel wanted those things which they should not or could not have. In the wilderness where GOD fed them manna and granted them meat from birds that HE provided for them;

they lusted after the food they did not have that they remembered in Egypt. Some even sought after other gods. Some lusted after and engaged in sex outside of marriage. Paul says of these things, "Neither let us tempt God." We should not be desiring acts of sin. We should not be fantasizing about those things which we know are against God's will and desire for us. For we open ourselves to destruction. Christ will never leave us. Yet opening yourself, your desires, and your lusts to things that are against God's will opens you to thinking about the things that are against God. How much closer are you to engaging those acts of sin, the more you think of them? Worse still, Christ equated our thoughts of sin with an act of sin. If we want to be HIS and do the things that please Christ, we must work towards thinking and desiring to please HIM above all else.

Dear Lord Jesus,

Please strengthen me in my weakness. Lord, help me to think and do the things which You have set for me to desire and to do. Lord, help me that my thoughts would be centered on following Your will. Lord, work on me. Change me so that my desires would forever be so that which You desire for me.

In Jesus name, Amen.

Day #44
I Corinthians 10:11-13

11 Now all these things happened unto them for examples: and they are written for our admonition, upon whom the ends of the world are come.
12 Wherefore let him that thinks he stands take heed lest he fall.
13 There hath no temptation taken you but such as is common to man: but God *is* faithful, who will not suffer you to be tempted above that you are able; but will with the temptation also make a way to escape, that you may be able to bear *it*.

We serve a God that allowed Himself to experience life as we do. He came in the person of Jesus and was tempted by the devil himself. Verse 12 hits at the heart of the man/woman he thinks that they are OKAY standing in their faith. When you stand, you must take care and pay attention because there are temptations. You must be wary. But that is all for nothing if your stand is not bolstered by your own delving into the Word of God for devotions/study on a daily basis.

You cannot successfully stand against temptation without knowing scriptural responses to those temptations. You do not need to quote scripture, but it can help! You need to know what the Bible says about those things. As believers, we have to desire God's will for us over our own. Add into this a nightly request before you close your eyes at night: "Lord please continue to mold me and make me after Your will."

Dear Lord Jesus,

May You be stronger in my today than yesterday. May I continually be strengthened by Your Word and love. Lord, You grant me many miracles each day. You do special things just to make me smile! You plan for me! I have so much to be thankful for. Lord, help me to resist those things that would pull me away from your desires for my life.

In Jesus name, Amen.

Day #45
I Corinthians 10:14-22

14   Wherefore, my dearly beloved, flee from idolatry.
15   I speak as to wise men; judge you what I say.
16   The cup of blessing which we bless, is it not the communion of the blood of Christ? The bread which we break, is it not the communion of the body of Christ?
17   For we *being* many are one bread, *and* one body: for we are all partakers of that one bread.
18   Behold Israel after the flesh: are not they which eat of the sacrifices partakers of the altar?
19   What say I then? that the idol is any thing, or that which is offered in sacrifice to idols is any thing?

20 But I *say*, that the things which the Gentiles sacrifice, they sacrifice to devils, and not to God: and I would not that you should have fellowship with devils.
21 You cannot drink the cup of the Lord, and the cup of devils: you cannot be partakers of the Lord's table, and of the table of devils.
22 Do we provoke the Lord to jealousy? are we stronger than he?

Paul reminds us that we as Christians have liberty, in that we know God and know that idols are false gods, more so they are demons pretending to be gods. We have freedom in our knowledge of God and in our relationship with the one true God.

Paul adds a reminder here that we as believers are one. We are a community of believers. We believe in Jesus Christ, the author and finisher of our faith. It is through HIS sacrifice that we are saved. It is through HIS work and HIS resurrection that we are actually accepted into the arms of the loving God. This was done for us. We did nothing to deserve this. NOTHING! We should not be finding reasons to separate. We should be seeing reasons why we should be joining in fellowship with our brothers and sisters in Christ.

Paul mentions here that we should not be having fellowship with disbelievers. Fellowship is communing together. It is one thing to do evangelism to bring others to Christ. It is OKAY for the lost to enter a church to find Christ. But they should not be counted as one with the church body. To do that allows them to proclaim and share their beliefs in your fellowship. They can see this as an opportunity to evangelize you towards whatever faith structure they want to share.

Dear Lord Jesus,

Your love is greater than any mountain, deeper than any ocean, and more desirable than a warm blanket on a cold night. Lord, you are there for me. You have watched over me. You have guided me even when I was not willing to listen to you. Lord, your encouragement of fellowship and your desire that it be with only those who share this love of You is filled with wisdom. Even in this You offer protection to us. Lord, may You truly be praised.

In Jesus name, Amen.

Day #46
I Corinthians 10:23-26

23   All things are lawful for me, but all things are not expedient: all things are lawful for me, but all things edify not.
24   Let no man seek his own, but every man another's *wealth*.
25   Whatsoever is sold in the shambles, *that* eat, asking no question for conscience sake:
26   For the earth *is* the Lord's, and the fulness thereof.

Paul is consistently reminding us that we have Christian liberty. But that does not mean we should do things without thinking of others. We should be examining whether our actions may or may not cause harm to new believers. We should be thinking not only of others is not an easy message. Too often that is our first and foremost thought—ME. We go straight from "I want," to "gimme now." That is the way of the world. It is not the way of Christ. Let us put others before our own selfishness.

Paul also speaks to the things sold at market or offered to you when you are guest. Some things you should take for granted.

Dear Lord Jesus,

I want to put others before me. I want to be the person who sees Your desires and will before I begin to seek that which I desire. Lord, use me, please. Use me as Your servant. Guide me in the way I should go. Help me so that I may be an example to others of Your great love.

In Jesus name, Amen.

Day #47
I Corinthians 10:27-33

27   If any of them that believe not bid you *to a feast*, and you be disposed to go; whatsoever is set before you, eat, asking no question for conscience sake.

28   But if any man say unto you, This is offered in sacrifice unto idols, eat not for his sake that shewed it, and for conscience sake: for the earth *is* the Lord's, and the fulness thereof:

29   Conscience, I say, not your own, but of the other: for why is my liberty judged of another *man's* conscience?

30   For if I by grace be a partaker, why am I evil spoken of for that for which I give thanks?
31   Whether therefore you eat, or drink, or whatsoever you do, do all to the glory of God.
32   Give none offence, neither to the Jews, nor to the Gentiles, nor to the church of God:
33   Even as I please all *men* in all *things*, not seeking mine own profit, but the *profit* of many, that they may be saved.

Paul speaks to the believer invited to an unbeliever's home. They should be grateful for what they receive. They should not ask questions. That will allow them to eat and drink. But if the host offers information such as the meat being offered to idols, then we as believers should not partake. Some Christians are against the consumption of alcoholic beverages. If a person with this belief went to an unbeliever's home and was offered a drink that had no indication it was alcoholic and the host informed him it was alcoholic, he may then say thank you and put the drink down. This action can be a testimony of keeping you separate from the world.

Yet, this type of choice is up to the Christian, as there are no set rules in the Bible on things like alcohol, with the exception of addressing drunkenness. The real test here is not whether as a believer you choose to say yes or no to whatever your host provides you. It is "Whether you eat, or drink, or whatsoever you do, are you able to do this to the glory of God?"

Dear Lord Jesus,

Your Word is a lamp onto my feet and a light unto my path. Lord, Your Word shows me if I am following Your path or not. It shines a light on the Way I should go. Lord, help me to so treasure

Your Word so that I can keep it in my heart so I may make those decisions I need to for so that I may say, "I do this for the glory of God." Lord help me to cut off those things in my life which I know are not to Your glory.

In Jesus name, Amen.

Day #48
I Corinthians 11:1

1   Be you followers of me, even as I also *am* of Christ.

This verse though small carries a heavy weight of truth. There are some pastors and teachers who would desire that you follow them and listen to them because of their claimed authority. Their claim being that they are God's man. They do not feel they can be questioned, or challenged. They wear Christ like an article of clothing rather than have Christ within them. These "men of God," do not quote this scripture, because it empowers the believers to look at a man's life who leads and ask that all important question, "Is this man of Christ?"

I once visited a church in the midst of one of the most impoverished neighborhoods in my city. People had entered and went outside. You could tell they were struggling financially by their appearance. Some wore that difficulty in their facial appearance. I just happened to be outside and saw the pastor arrive late. The service was to begin in the next ten minutes. He parked his luxury vehicle in a spot designated for him. Got out in his designer suit, and stepped towards the church in his designer shoes, with his hair slicked back in his expensive haircut. This man deserved to have his life looked at to see if he was "also of Christ."

Dear Lord Jesus,

Thank you for expecting us to look for You in the lives of those who would lead us. Thank you for granting us that freedom and liberty. Though there are some who would claim their authority cannot be questioned, You gave us something to measure whether that authority should be questioned at all. Lord, I ask that strengthen those in leadership roles in our churches. Lord, that You would strengthen them in their roles as father and husband. Lord, that You would strengthen their ability to live for You and give them the opportunity to study that they may share with us. Lord, may they truly be examples of Your great love.

In Jesus name, Amen.

Day #49
I Corinthians 11:2-16

2   Now I praise you, brethren, that you remember me in all things, and keep the ordinances, as I delivered *them* to you.
3   But I would have you know, that the head of every man is Christ; and the head of the woman *is* the man; and the head of Christ *is* God.
4   Every man praying or prophesying, having *his* head covered, dishonours his head.

5	But every woman that prays or prophesies with *her* head uncovered dishonours her head: for that is even all one as if she were shaven.
6	For if the woman be not covered, let her also be shorn: but if it be a shame for a woman to be shorn or shaven, let her be covered.
7	For a man indeed ought not to cover *his* head, forasmuch as he is the image and glory of God: but the woman is the glory of the man.
8	For the man is not of the woman; but the woman of the man.
9	Neither was the man created for the woman; but the woman for the man.
10	For this cause ought the woman to have power on *her* head because of the angels.
11	Nevertheless neither is the man without the woman, neither the woman without the man, in the Lord.
12	For as the woman *is* of the man, even so *is* the man also by the woman; but all things of God.
13	Judge in yourselves: is it comely that a woman pray unto God uncovered?
14	Does not even nature itself teach you, that, if a man have long hair, it is a shame unto him?
15	But if a woman have long hair, it is a glory to her: for *her* hair is given her for a covering.
16	But if any man seem to be contentious, we have no such custom, neither the churches of God.

Paul speaks to order in the order of the church. Christ being the head, the man is next and the woman follows. He then begins to talk about hair and covering of the head with respect to the customs of the people. He maintains the order given by God requiring God be first, man second, and the woman submit to the man also.

His references to a woman wearing a head covering are nothing similar to Islam's god wanting women to wear a hijab. The women had no choice under this faith, and its purpose was a declaration of who the women were to warn the male followers of Islam.

But in the case of what Paul is discussing here, he is backing up local customs of women wearing head coverings. He does not discourage it because it also agrees with Biblical teachings on order in the church at that time.

Today, most women in America do not wear head coverings when outside. So, this ordinance or rule would not be relevant since it is a reference to the local dress and customs of the day.

Dear Lord Jesus,

You are the GREAT I AM. You know us inside and out. You seek out our hearts and minds. You know our thoughts and desires. Lord, work on me. Help me that I may be one who is seen as Yours and is able to show others Your great love.

In Jesus name, Amen.

Day #50
I Corinthians 11:17-22

17   Now in this that I declare *unto you* I praise *you* not, that you come together not for the better, but for the worse.

18   For first of all, when you come together in the church, I hear that there be divisions among you; and I partly believe it.

19   For there must be also heresies among you, that they which are approved may be made manifest among you.

20   When you come together therefore into one place, *this* is not to eat the Lord's supper.

21   For in eating every one taketh before *other* his own supper: and one is hungry, and another is drunken.

22   What? have you not houses to eat and to drink in? or despise you the church of God, and shame them that have not? What shall I say to you? shall I praise you in this? I praise *you* not.

If you are having some difficulty grasping this passage, think of a church picnic where each family brings their own food and drink. Some bring things like alcoholic beverages and get drunk. Some bring gourmet meals, and some bring nothing for they have nothing. No one offers the poor anything. There is no unity. This picnic of persons is united only in the concept that this is a type of party setting. Some even bring to share things that are not in agreement with the Bible and hope to sow these things.

We do not need to have the Lord's Supper every time we gather, but we should be making our gatherings about Christ and not about ourselves. We should be engaging in fellowship, valuing the time we have with others, sharing, helping, lifting up each other, and foremost, we should be worshipping Christ together.

Dear Lord Jesus,

    I pray for my church. Lord, not for the building but for those of us who make up the church. Please, Lord strengthen each of us in You. Lord, encourage each and every believer that they may not only praise You and lift You up but that they may take Your Word and have it blossom and thrive in their hearts each and every day. Lord, I also ask for a special blessing on our leaders. Lord, strengthen and solidify their families in You. Protect them because they provide teachings about You and examples of how we should be pursuing You, the Great and Living GOD!

In Jesus name, Amen.

Day #51
I Corinthians 11:23-34

23   For I have received of the Lord that which also I delivered unto you, That the Lord Jesus the *same* night in which he was betrayed took bread:

24   And when he had given thanks, he brake *it*, and said, Take, eat: this is my body, which is broken for you: this do in remembrance of me.

25   After the same manner also *he took* the cup, when he had supped, saying, This cup is the new testament in my blood: this do you, as oft as you drink *it*, in remembrance of me.

26   For as often as you eat this bread, and drink this cup, you do shew the Lord's death till he come.

27 Wherefore whosoever shall eat this bread, and drink *this* cup of the Lord, unworthily, shall be guilty of the body and blood of the Lord.
28 But let a man examine himself, and so let him eat of *that* bread, and drink of *that* cup.
29 For he that eats and drinks unworthily, eats and drinks damnation to himself, not discerning the Lord's body.
30 For this cause many *are* weak and sickly among you, and many sleep.
31 For if we would judge ourselves, we should not be judged.
32 But when we are judged, we are chastened of the Lord, that we should not be condemned with the world.
33 Wherefore, my brethren, when you come together to eat, tarry one for another.
34 And if any man hunger, let him eat at home; that you come not together unto condemnation. And the rest will I set in order when I come.

    This is the most extensive passage outside of the Gospels on the Lord's Supper. J. Vernon McGee tells us that Paul reveals that there are three time elements to the ritual of the Lord's Supper. The Lord's Supper looks to the past, it reminds us of what the Lord has done for us on the cross (vs. 24-25). It speaks to the present, that we engage in this ritual that reminds us of who Christ IS and what HE has done. That we should continue to do this with our fellow believers when we gather (vs. 26). It also looks to the future. We should be partaking in the Lord's Supper "until He comes." Yes, thinking of what Christ did on the cross, sacrificing HIS life that we may have life is a sadness. But it is joy also, because of that work we have everlasting life with our Creator and Savior! Even better still, we know HE is coming again!

All the more reason that this ritual this act of engaging in reminding of who Christ was, what He has done, and his return is not something we should do lightly. It is not something we should invite disbelievers into. It is something beyond their comprehension. How can they comprehend this when they do not have the spirit of Christ within themselves to experience this personally? It becomes nothing more than a ritual. In truth, the Lord's Supper is something personal. It is something we can experience deep within us. We can experience sorrow, judgement, and joy based on where we are in our relationship with Christ.

Dear Lord Jesus,

Help me to be one whose love of You is never hidden. Lord, may I point the way to Your great love for us. May I be one whose words and actions speak to others as a person who knows YOU personally and has a reason to share that love. Lord, direct my words so that I may plant seeds of that love in those who do not yet know You.

In Jesus name, Amen.

Day #52
I Corinthians 12:1-3

1   Now concerning spiritual *gifts*, brethren, I would not have you ignorant.

2   You know that you were Gentiles, carried away unto these dumb idols, even as you were led.

3   Wherefore I give you to understand, that no man speaking by the Spirit of God calleth Jesus accursed: and *that* no man can say that Jesus is the Lord, but by the Holy Ghost.

Chapter twelve begins the second division of 1 Corinthians. The first eleven chapters address carnalities. Chapter 12 starts the section on spiritualities. Paul seems to relish this change to spiritual things in verse 1.

The Corinthians were polytheists. They worshipped idols. Impersonal gods. Some whom history may have recorded as once being men. But stone idols and wood idols cannot speak, they do not interact with anyone. Their gods were so inferior to a God who loves and seeks after individuals. Yet, because God seeks the heart of the individual, He gives them a choice to hear who HE is and to respond to it with a choice to seek HIM out or not.

In verse 3, simple truths are exposed. They are so simple you wonder if they are not known and how they could not be known. A Christian would never refer to Christ as accursed, and a non-believer would not call Christ HIS Lord.

I have met men who pursue a false god named Allah. Some of those were willing to say things to deceive me into believing that their god accepted Jesus as lord. This was a lie. This faith structure encourages deceit to bring people into their faith. You can lie about anything to bring people in. But faith in Christ is about the light of truth. It is in the God who is TRUTH!

Saying Jesus is Lord is through the Holy Spirit. BELIEVING it and living it is life-changing!

Dear Lord Jesus,

Help me to grow spiritually. Strengthen me. Work on me that my time in prayer and in Your Word would build up in my heart and mind. Lord, I want to be more like You. Lord, I desire to hear your voice and feel your touch on my life. I know you are not finished with me. Thank you for not giving up on me.

In Jesus name, Amen.

Day #53
I Corinthians 12:4-11

4   Now there are diversities of gifts, but the same Spirit.
5   And there are differences of administrations, but the same Lord.
6   And there are diversities of operations, but it is the same God which worketh all in all.
7   But the manifestation of the Spirit is given to every man to profit withal.
8   For to one is given by the Spirit the word of wisdom; to another the word of knowledge by the same Spirit;
9   To another faith by the same Spirit; to another the gifts of healing by the same Spirit;
10 To another the working of miracles; to another prophecy; to another discerning of spirits; to another *divers* kinds of tongues; to another the interpretation of tongues:
11 But all these worketh that one and the selfsame Spirit, dividing to every man severally as he will.

Some may place limits on the Holy Spirit. Limiting God is nothing but wrong. The diverse gifts, here spoken of by Paul, all come from God. They are not all given to everyone. But they are given out individually to whom God will, that all may profit from. This can be seen as God knowing His creation of man. We will walk past those who do not offer things to us and who can profit us in some way. But by His dispersing the gifts of the Spirit like this, we should communicate more, we should work together, and we should function as a unit. This creates a unity of believers.

Some may make bold claims limiting God's ability to continue to disperse these gifts today. But Paul makes no such claim. Not here, that is for sure. The gifts of the Spirit, if anything proclaims to the believer and to the non-believer, that Our God, Jesus, is the God who does impossible things! These gifts are reasons to worship and praise HIS name. These gifts are dispersed by God on us, the lowly creation, whom God loves so much He came to save us! These gifts are for the "joint-heirs of Christ." They are a proclamation to the one that believes and receives, that "YES, God sees me as an individual, Yes God loves even me. Yes, God has given even me a gift."

Dear Lord Jesus,

May You be praised above the heavens. You came down and died for us that we maybe come joint-heirs with You. Your gifts of the spirit demonstrate your unending love toward us like a flood of glad tidings. Lord, use me and the gifts You have given me. Use me to point the way to that incredible love that claimed me!

In Jesus name, Amen.

Day #54
I Corinthians 12:12-26

12 For as the body is one, and hath many members, and all the members of that one body, being many, are one body: so also *is* Christ.
13 For by one Spirit are we all baptized into one body, whether *we be* Jews or Gentiles, whether *we be* bond or free; and have been all made to drink into one Spirit.
14 For the body is not one member, but many.
15 If the foot shall say, Because I am not the hand, I am not of the body; is it therefore not of the body?
16 And if the ear shall say, Because I am not the eye, I am not of the body; is it therefore not of the body?
17 If the whole body *were* an eye, where *were* the hearing? If the whole *were* hearing, where *were* the smelling?
18 But now hath God set the members every one of them in the body, as it hath pleased him.
19 And if they were all one member, where *were* the body?
20 But now *are they* many members, yet but one body.
21 And the eye cannot say unto the hand, I have no need of you: nor again the head to the feet, I have no need of you.
22 Nay, much more those members of the body, which seem to be more feeble, are necessary:
23 And those *members* of the body, which we think to be less honourable, upon these we bestow more abundant honour; and our uncomely *parts* have more abundant comeliness.

24   For our comely *parts* have no need: but God hath tempered the body together, having given more abundant honour to that *part* which lacked:
25   That there should be no schism in the body; but *that* the members should have the same care one for another.
26   And whether one member suffer, all the members suffer with it; or one member be honoured, all the members rejoice with it.

The church has many members. Paul emphasizes this repeatedly throughout this passage. We are different. We have our own gifts from God. We have different roles and tasks. Yet, we function as one body.

I broke my foot when I was younger and was showing off for my son playing basketball. I felt the bone snap. I knew something was wrong. Yet the medical advice I received after X-rays was that it was just a sprain. So, I walked on it until the pain was so bad I went to another doctor. This time the doctor who read the X-rays said I now had three breaks because I had broken one bone and as a result of not taking care of it, two other bones broke.

We are one body. When an area within our body is hurting we should provide care and help. When an area of our body is rejoicing we should share in that joy. We need to support each other. The different gifts God gives compliment the others. Together as a church body, it strengthens and lifts up.

Dear Lord Jesus,

Help me to lift up and encourage my brothers and sisters in the church. Help me to see what I can do to strengthen the unity within the body of Christ. Lord, use me, for I am Yours.

In Jesus name, Amen.

Day #55
I Corinthians 12:27-31

27 Now you are the body of Christ, and members in particular.
28 And God hath set some in the church, first apostles, secondarily prophets, thirdly teachers, after that miracles, then gifts of healings, helps, governments, diversities of tongues.
29 *Are* all apostles? *are* all prophets? *are* all teachers? *are* all workers of miracles?
30 Have all the gifts of healing? do all speak with tongues? do all interpret?
31 But covet earnestly the best gifts: and yet shew I unto you a more excellent way.

Paul keeps reminding us of the importance of the unity of Christ. He also speaks to the order in the church of gifts and offices. Some in Corinth were allowing vanity and jealousy to enter their hearts about spiritual gifts and offices. Wherever these two evils are they work to destroy from within. Paul answers these difficulties with verse 31. "Seek the best gifts." How do you do this? Pursue a deeper relationship with Christ. Matthew Henry put it this way: "True charity is greatly to be preferred to the most glorious gifts. To have the heart glow with mutual love is vastly better than to glare with the most pompous titles, offices, or powers."

Dear Lord Jesus,

I desire spiritual gifts that I do not yet have. Lord, help me to grow in my relationship with You. Lord, bring me to a deeper relationship with You. Lord, I desire to be more loving, and more knowledgeable of Your Word. More of a person who can share You with others. Lord, use me.

In Jesus name, Amen.

Day #56
I Corinthians 13:1-3

1 Though I speak with the tongues of men and of angels, and have not charity, I am become *as* sounding brass, or a tinkling cymbal.
2 And though I have *the gift of* prophecy, and understand all mysteries, and all knowledge; and though I have all faith, so that I could remove mountains, and have not charity, I am nothing.

3 And though I bestow all my goods to feed *the poor*, and though I give my body to be burned, and have not charity, it profits me nothing.

 J. Vernon McGee says of the lack of charity, which also means love, sounding like brass, or a tinkling cymbal in verse 1:

> "I am nothing in this world but a noisy bell. And this is the act of the emotions of the heart here. Language without love is like noise without melody is the way Dr. Scroggy put it, or as McGee puts it chatter without charity. Sound without soul. You can sing like a Seraph and without love, it is nothing but the hiss of hell. Love is what gives meaning and depth and reality and makes it meaningful."

 I once knew an incredible violinist. Her form was perfect, she could compete and get the highest positions in any orchestra. But she was lacking in understanding of who Christ is and his saving grace. I felt that missing in her beautiful playing. It surprised me. I remember the first day that hit me. Then I had no clue what it was that was off in her playing. Her notes were perfect. Her tone was 100 percent on. Her timing was perfect. Yet, she did not know the joy of the love of Christ. I remember figuring that out and being surprised I could feel that.

 People there is something incredible in fellowship with other believers. There is a love that binds them together. In such a place the lack of love is loud and noisy announcing your entrance. It may not be seen or words or deeds, but it is felt regardless.

Dear Lord Jesus,

Help me Lord to love as never before. Help me to give up all, that I might love beyond what I know today. You are the God who does impossible things. Help me to grow, help me to reach and share that wondrous love today.

In Jesus name, Amen.

Day #57
I Corinthians 13:4-7

4   Charity suffers long, *and* is kind; charity envies not; charity vaunts not itself, is not puffed up,
5   Doth not behave itself unseemly, seeks not her own, is not easily provoked, thinketh no evil;
6   Rejoices not in iniquity, but rejoices in the truth;
7   Bears all things, believeth all things, hopes all things, endures all things.

Paul continues to talk about love. Charity being love. The positive side being shown in verse 4. It suffers, is kind, it does not envy. It does not vaunt itself, nor is it puffed up. When we think of these things these are all the things we look for when we look for someone to admire. Sadly, when we get to know that person well, some of these positives usually fade away.

In verse 5, we have the "negative" of love. That negative is in truth a positive. It does not behave badly. It does not seek its own interests. It is not easily provoked. Love doing these things does NO evil. It bears all things, believes all things. It is trusting. It hopes for good things! It endures the world for Christ.

Dear Lord Jesus,

You are my hope. You are the reason I love. For You first loved me. You have taught me much about love far beyond my experiences. Your love is beyond my comprehension. It is overpowering, comforting and it brings joy and hope for what is to come! Lord for all these wondrous examples of what Your love does. Please use me to share that wondrous truth.

In Jesus name, Amen.

Day #58
I Corinthians 13:8-10

8   Charity never fails: but whether *there be* prophecies, they shall fail; whether *there be* tongues, they shall cease; whether *there be* knowledge, it shall vanish away.
9   For we know in part, and we prophesy in part.
10   But when that which is perfect is come, then that which is in part shall be done away.

Paul is speaking about gifts passing away. Some take this to mean that these gifts have already have their time. That there are no longer gifts like tongues, prophecy, word of knowledge and more. BUT, when you read verse 10, it speaks to this happening when Christ returns. This is something yet to happen. Perfection has not come because Christ has yet to return. This passage refers to his being present on earth. Not in the clouds. Should we be thankful for these gifts, yes. Should we desire these gifts, YES! Should we believe those who state they no longer exist, NO! The answer to the time these gifts passing away is here.

Dear Lord Jesus,

You are the LIVING GOD! You exemplify love. Your words, Your actions, and Your love for me are beyond comprehension. Lord, you care for us so much that You gave us gifts. Lord, strengthen us and embolden us to share Your love.

In Jesus name, Amen.

Day #59
I Corinthians 13:11-13

11   When I was a child, I spoke as a child, I understood as a child, I thought as a child: but when I became a man, I put away childish things.

12   For now we see through a glass, darkly; but then face to face: now I know in part; but then shall I know even as also I am known.

13   And now abides faith, hope, charity, these three; but the greatest of these *is* charity.

When all is said and done with our time on this earth, we will see things differently. We will see this as a time we were foolish. We will see this time as childish. We may not truly know what is to come, but we do know that Jesus is there as He is there for us. We know that He told us there are many mansions. We hold to this with faith, hope, and love. Christ being the full embodiment of love when he was here walking amongst us, and after He was risen He continues to be that perfect love. Without Him, we have no faith or hope. Without Him, there is no love that gives unselfishly beyond our understanding. For God first loved us. We learned to be unselfish because of HIS love.

Dear Lord Jesus,

Your love exceeds any borders are barriers. It overwhelms It expands to take more and more in to its arms. Lord, Your love is the greatest, because You loved even me in my sin. You even love me so much You continue to work on me, making me better. Lord, use me to share Your wondrous love with others.

In Jesus name, Amen.

Day #60
I Corinthians 14:1-5

1 Follow after charity, and desire spiritual *gifts*, but rather that you may prophesy.
2 For he that speaks in an *unknown* tongue speaks not unto men, but unto God: for no man understands *him*; howbeit in the spirit he speaks mysteries.
3 But he that prophesies speaks unto men *to* edification, and exhortation, and comfort.
4 He that speaks in an *unknown* tongue edifies himself; but he that prophesies edifies the church.
5 I would that you all spoke with tongues, but rather that you prophesied: for greater *is* he that prophesies than he that speaks with tongues, except he interpret, that the church may receive edifying.

Paul continues the superiority of love theme as he starts to talk about the superiority of gifts compared to speaking in tongues. This is a gift of God. It is not something taught. It is language that bubbles up in joy and speaks words we do not know in praise and adoration to the Jesus Christ our Lord. Put together with the gift of interpretation the pairing create prophecies. Spiritual gifts are powerful! Even the least of them, tongues edifies the individual and builds that person up. But these are not things for bragging and boasting. They are for your prayer time in private or amongst gatherings of fellow believers. This gift that lifts up you is not to be used to boast or brag. It must be used with humility to praise the living God. Yet, it is the least of the spiritual gifts. So, to desire more spiritual gifts is not wrong. It is something to do.

Dear Lord Jesus,

I thank You for the gifts You have given me. Lord, You give me gifts even though You are still working on me and molding me into something better. Lord, I ask that You would grant me more spiritual gifts so that I may bless others with Your wondrous love.

In Jesus name, Amen.

Day #61
I Corinthians 14:6-19

6   Now, brethren, if I come unto you speaking with tongues, what shall I profit you, except I shall speak to you either by revelation, or by knowledge, or by prophesying, or by doctrine?

7   And even things without life giving sound, whether pipe or harp, except they give a distinction in the sounds, how shall it be known what is piped or harped?

8   For if the trumpet give an uncertain sound, who shall prepare himself to the battle?

9   So likewise you, except you utter by the tongue words easy to be understood, how shall it be known what is spoken? for you shall speak into the air.

10	There are, it may be, so many kinds of voices in the world, and none of them *is* without signification.
11	Therefore if I know not the meaning of the voice, I shall be unto him that speaks a barbarian, and he that speaks *shall be* a barbarian unto me.
12	Even so you, forasmuch as you are zealous of spiritual *gifts*, seek that you may excel to the edifying of the church.
13	Wherefore let him that speaks in an *unknown* tongue pray that he may interpret.
14	For if I pray in an *unknown* tongue, my spirit prays, but my understanding is unfruitful.
15	What is it then? I will pray with the spirit, and I will pray with the understanding also: I will sing with the spirit, and I will sing with the understanding also.
16	Else when you shall bless with the spirit, how shall he that occupies the room of the unlearned say Amen at your giving of thanks, seeing he understands not what you sayest?
17	For you verily give thanks well, but the other is not edified.
18	I thank my God, I speak with tongues more than you all:
19	Yet in the church I had rather speak five words with my understanding, that *by my voice* I might teach others also, than ten thousand words in an *unknown* tongue.

In the early church the gift of tongues was known and was practiced often. Paul writes of this gift to encourage seeking better spiritual gifts. Yet, he speaks glowingly of this gift of tongues. He says of this gift, "when he speaks in tongues, his spirit prays." You may be blessed through this gift but unless others in the room know the language no one else is blessed. Paul tells us we should seek spiritual gifts not for ourselves also, but that the church body may benefit.

With this said, I marvel that so many churches hid the gift of tongues from their sheep. I grew up in such a church. The concept of tongues and other spiritual gifts was never mentioned. They always skipped over passages like this. Why? Could it be that passages like this encourage us to grow in Christ and to seek spiritual gifts? That these gifts are for everyone not just those in leadership roles? Whatever the reason, we should not hide the gifts God gave us. But we should use them as God directs us. Paul here tells us that there is a time for sharing this gift.

Dear Lord Jesus,

You give us ways to glorify You that also, through the gift of tongues, lift us up too. It's impossible to explain, but it is true. Lord, praising Your name through worship and through speaking tongues always leaves us feeling better. Lord, I thank you for this gift. Please, Lord, I ask for more gifts from You that my church may be lifted and up and that my brothers and sisters in Christ may benefit.

In Jesus name, Amen.

Day #62
I Corinthians 14:20-30

20	Brethren, be not children in understanding: howbeit in malice be you children, but in understanding be men.

21 In the law it is written, With *men of* other tongues and other lips will I speak unto this people; and yet for all that will they not hear me, saith the Lord.

22 Wherefore tongues are for a sign, not to them that believe, but to them that believe not: but prophesying *serves* not for them that believe not, but for them which believe.

23 If therefore the whole church be come together into one place, and all speak with tongues, and there come in *those that are* unlearned, or unbelievers, will they not say that you are mad?

24 But if all prophesy, and there come in one that believeth not, or *one* unlearned, he is convinced of all, he is judged of all:

25 And thus are the secrets of his heart made manifest; and so falling down on *his* face he will worship God, and report that God is in you of a truth.

26 How is it then, brethren? when you come together, every one of you hath a psalm, hath a doctrine, hath a tongue, hath a revelation, hath an interpretation. Let all things be done unto edifying.

27 If any man speak in an *unknown* tongue, *let it be* by two, or at the most *by* three, and *that* by course; and let one interpret.

28 But if there be no interpreter, let him keep silence in the church; and let him speak to himself, and to God.

29 Let the prophets speak two or three, and let the other judge.

Paul here is speaking to order in the church. There is a place for the gift of tongues but it is not for all in meetings where those who may not know Christ are present. Tongues edify the believer, not the unbeliever, whereas prophecy, even the interpretation of tongues can also edify the unbeliever to a conviction of his/her sin that repentance becomes their foremost need as they give their life to Christ. But a place where many speak in tongues could cause the unbeliever to think of the church as a place of madness. If tongues are a gift that edifies the one with the gift, gatherings where unbelievers are present are not the correct place. Yes, the gift of tongues, has its place in worship. But it is better that opportunity is given to praise the Creator of all in our own tongues that those who do not yet know Him may find Christ. This is the reason for the guidelines Paul gives in verse 27.

Dear Lord Jesus,

Thank you for the pastors and preachers who share Your Word so that we might be blessed with the wisdom in Your Word. Lord, please bless these men, not only for preaching Your Word but for keeping order in the church. Lord, I ask that You lift up those who are used to sharing Christ with others. Lord, I pray that those who share Christ with the lost will see the fruit of their labor.

In Jesus name, Amen.

Day #63
I Corinthians 14:30-40

30   If *any thing* be revealed to another that sits by, let the first hold his peace.

31	For you may all prophesy one by one, that all may learn, and all may be comforted.
32	And the spirits of the prophets are subject to the prophets.
33	For God is not *the author* of confusion, but of peace, as in all churches of the saints.
34	Let your women keep silence in the churches: for it is not permitted unto them to speak; but *they are commanded* to be under obedience, as also saith the law.
35	And if they will learn any thing, let them ask their husbands at home: for it is a shame for women to speak in the church.
36	What? came the word of God out from you? or came it unto you only?
37	If any man think himself to be a prophet, or spiritual, let him acknowledge that the things that I write unto you are the commandments of the Lord.
38	But if any man be ignorant, let him be ignorant.
39	Wherefore, brethren, covet to prophesy, and forbid not to speak with tongues.
40	Let all things be done decently and in order.

The last passage of chapter 14 here has to do with "things being done decently and in order" in the church. Just as with the gift of tongues having order, there is an order for prophets and there is order for women.

In verse 30, prophesying is shown as not sharing something that is known.

The verses on women keeping silent in the church in the midst of speaking of spiritual gifts may refer to women using spiritual gifts in the church.

Paul also speaks about allowing people to make their own choices. Ignorance is a willful lack of knowledge. If someone chooses not to know something we cannot force that knowledge on them.

Dear Lord Jesus,

You are a God of order. You used Paul to show us order in a church. Lord, help us to seek Your glory. That You alone may be praised. Help us to seek Your glory not our own by maintaining Your order in the church.

In Jesus name, Amen.

Day #64
I Corinthians 15:1-11

1 Moreover, brethren, I declare unto you the gospel which I preached unto you, which also you have received, and wherein you stand;
2 By which also you are saved, if you keep in memory what I preached unto you, unless you have believed in vain.
3 For I delivered unto you first of all that which I also received, how that Christ died for our sins according to the scriptures;
4 And that he was buried, and that he rose again the third day according to the scriptures:
5 And that he was seen of Cephas, then of the twelve:

6	After that, he was seen of above five hundred brethren at once; of whom the greater part remain unto this present, but some are fallen asleep.
7	After that, he was seen of James; then of all the apostles.
8	And last of all he was seen of me also, as of one born out of due time.
9	For I am the least of the apostles, that am not meet to be called an apostle, because I persecuted the church of God.
10	But by the grace of God I am what I am: and his grace which *was bestowed* upon me was not in vain; but I laboured more abundantly than they all: yet not I, but the grace of God which was with me.
11	Therefore whether *it were* I or they, so we preach, and so you believed.

Paul is telling us that there is no Gospel, no Good News apart from the death and RESSURECTION of Jesus Christ! This gospel is a truth, a message that Paul was not the first to receive. In many ways, he was the least of the Apostles. Paul was not with Jesus as he lived and breathed teaching his disciples. Nor does he claim to be present at the death of Christ. He lauds those who knew of the risen Lord before himself. This is important. Why? Because today, there are people out there who claim Paul was the inventor of Christianity. There are actually High School Social Studies textbooks out there with this claim written into them. I have seen at least one of them. Paul was not the first to proclaim the resurrection of Jesus. He gives Peter credit for having been the first. Paul goes on and speaks of 500 more who knew the risen Lord Jesus before he did. Paul may appear to have had a larger footprint in time, from his work sharing the Gospel, but as he states, he was not the first.

Yet, it does not matter who was first, or last to believe, it matters that the risen Lord Jesus was preached and that you believe!

Dear Lord Jesus,

You first loved us. You came to show us how to live and then died taking the burden of our sins upon yourself. Your resurrection proclaims YOUR glory! This is good news we all must share. Lord embolden me. Use me to share this great news of what you have done for us.

In Jesus name, Amen.

Day #65
I Corinthians 15:2-19

12   Now if Christ be preached that he rose from the dead, how say some among you that there is no resurrection of the dead?
13   But if there be no resurrection of the dead, then is Christ not risen:
14   And if Christ be not risen, then *is* our preaching vain, and your faith *is* also vain.
15   Yea, and we are found false witnesses of God; because we have testified of God that he raised up Christ: whom he raised not up, if so be that the dead rise not.
16   For if the dead rise not, then is not Christ raised:

17   And if Christ be not raised, your faith *is* vain; you are yet in your sins.
18   Then they also which are fallen asleep in Christ are perished.
19   If in this life only we have hope in Christ, we are of all men most miserable.

Paul spoke to those who were "most learned," the academics, the people puffed up with knowledge that told them no one could come back from the dead. Paul was dealing with skeptics on this topic and gave the "what if" scenarios.

Christianity is entirely based on the ability of God, himself, to do impossible things. These things are not based on man's ability. They are based on the Creator's ability! "IF CHRIST HAVE NOT RISEN, THEN ... IS YOUR FAITH IN VAIN." The truth is that Christians have HOPE! Christians look forward to the impossible things God can do instead of accepting the way things are. Christians look forward to the day when they can see their loved ones in Christ who have passed from this world. Christians look forward to meeting their Lord, Jesus! Some may call the resurrection of the dead impossible. Well, Paul here is saying their god is too small. Their god cannot do impossible things. But JESUS... JESUS did raise from the dead and we as believers are not miserable but we live on with the hope and promise that we are saved from our sins by what the Lord God has done for us because HE first loved us!

Dear Lord Jesus,

You are the God that does impossible things. You are the God who loves beyond our understanding. Without You we have no reason to hope and no reason to look forward to greater things in the hereafter. Your love – is overwhelming. It cleanses, it frees us from the weight of our sin. Lord, may YOU be praised for the wondrous things You have done for me. Lord, I ask that You call _____, _____, and _____ to be Yours also. Lord help them to find You. Help them to see the promises You keep!

In Jesus name, Amen.

Day #66
I Corinthians 15:20-28

20 But now is Christ risen from the dead, *and* become the firstfruits of them that slept.
21 For since by man *came* death, by man *came* also the resurrection of the dead.
22 For as in Adam all die, even so in Christ shall all be made alive.
23 But every man in his own order: Christ the firstfruits; afterward they that are Christ's at his coming.
24 Then *comes* the end, when he shall have delivered up the kingdom to God, even the Father; when he shall have put down all rule and all authority and power.
25 For he must reign, till he hath put all enemies under his feet.
26 The last enemy *that* shall be destroyed *is* death.

27   For he hath put all things under his feet. But when he saith all things are put under *him, it is* manifest that he is excepted, which did put all things under him.

28   And when all things shall be subdued unto him, then shall the Son also himself be subject unto him that put all things under him, that God may be all in all.

The "what ifs" are over and Paul writes these verses like a victory dance! These verse proclaim the victory of Christ, as the God who does impossible things! The victory of Christ in the resurrection of the dead becomes our victory! Not through anything we did, but all because of HIM! This victory and the coming day when death itself is subjected to Christ and placed under his feet are truly reasons to celebrate!

Dear Lord Jesus,

May you be praised for the incredible things You have done! Your resurrection, Your victory has become our victory. Lord, we are thankful for all You have done. Lord may we never forget what You have done for us. That You paid a price for us. That you beat death and rose from the dead. Lord, may we not forget that You are still battling for us as Your enemies are being made into Your footstool till even death shall be the last placed under Your foot. Praise YOU, Lord God, for all that You have done and will do.

In Jesus name, Amen.

Day #67
I Corinthians 15:29-38

29 Else what shall they do which are baptized for the dead, if the dead rise not at all? why are they then baptized for the dead?
30 And why stand we in jeopardy every hour?
31 I protest by your rejoicing which I have in Christ Jesus our Lord, I die daily.
32 If after the manner of men I have fought with beasts at Ephesus, what advantages it me, if the dead rise not? let us eat and drink; for tomorrow we die.
33 Be not deceived: evil communications corrupt good manners.
34 Awake to righteousness, and sin not; for some have not the knowledge of God: I speak *this* to your shame.
35 But some *man* will say, How are the dead raised up? and with what body do they come?
36 *You* fool, that which you sow is not quickened, except it die:
37 And that which you sow, you sow not that body that shall be, but bare grain, it may chance of wheat, or of some other *grain*:
38 But God giveth it a body as it hath pleased him, and to every seed his own body.

Paul looks at baptism in verse 29 in a manner that seems odd. We are baptized because Christ died for us. But---baptism is not complete without rising from the water, which is representative of HIS resurrection. He goes on to speak of the dangers he faced sharing Christ. Why should he face those dangers of Christ be not raised? Paul breaks it down to examples in nature that show the dead can rise. A seed is dead. It does not breathe. Yet we bury it expecting it to come to life. That seed which was dead becomes something new and living! God does the same with us.

Dear Lord Jesus,

You are the God who does impossible things. You set things in motions leaving little hints of Your coming work from the foundation of the earth. The planting of seeds spoken of in Genesis is shown as representative of having faith in Your resurrection! Lord thank you for showing us there are simple things in nature that display Your work and show us we should indeed have faith in You!

In Jesus name, Amen.

Day #68
I Corinthians 15:39-49

39 All flesh *is* not the same flesh: but *there is* one *kind of* flesh of men, another flesh of beasts, another of fishes, *and* another of birds.
40 *There are* also celestial bodies, and bodies terrestrial: but the glory of the celestial *is* one, and the *glory* of the terrestrial *is* another.

41 *There is* one glory of the sun, and another glory of the moon, and another glory of the stars: for *one* star differs from *another* star in glory.
42 So also *is* the resurrection of the dead. It is sown in corruption; it is raised in incorruption:
43 It is sown in dishonour; it is raised in glory: it is sown in weakness; it is raised in power:
44 It is sown a natural body; it is raised a spiritual body. There is a natural body, and there is a spiritual body.
45 And so it is written, The first man Adam was made a living soul; the last Adam *was made* a quickening spirit.
46 Howbeit that *was* not first which is spiritual, but that which is natural; and afterward that which is spiritual.
47 The first man *is* of the earth, earthy: the second man *is* the Lord from heaven.
48 As *is* the earthy, such *are* they also that are earthy: and as *is* the heavenly, such *are* they also that are heavenly.
49 And as we have borne the image of the earthy, we shall also bear the image of the heavenly.

Paul here shows he has a broad education. He understands many things and how those many things speak of the glory of God in the resurrection of the body. Today, we might say something dies because it is defective. But, when it is raised up, when that body is resurrected it is raised in perfection.

Not long ago, Christian children sang a song, "Bullfrogs and Butterflies, both been born again." There is sadness in the silence of the metamorphism. But there is JOY in the moment of the resurrection! That song about Bullfrogs and butterflies bubbles with the hope and joy we have in Christ.

Dear Lord Jesus,

You plan so far ahead for me, I thank you for all that You have done and will do for me. Lord, help me to share this joy and hope of knowing You. Lord, put me in a place to share Your glory that Your wonder, Your glory may be known.

In Jesus name, Amen.

Day #69
I Corinthians 15:50-58

50 Now this I say, brethren, that flesh and blood cannot inherit the kingdom of God; neither doth corruption inherit incorruption.
51 Behold, I shew you a mystery; We shall not all sleep, but we shall all be changed,
52 In a moment, in the twinkling of an eye, at the last trump: for the trumpet shall sound, and the dead shall be raised incorruptible, and we shall be changed.
53 For this corruptible must put on incorruption, and this mortal *must* put on immortality.
54 So when this corruptible shall have put on incorruption, and this mortal shall have put on immortality, then shall be brought to pass the saying that is written, Death is swallowed up in victory.
55 O death, where *is* your sting? O grave, where *is* your victory?
56 The sting of death *is* sin; and the strength of sin *is* the law.

57 But thanks *be* to God, which gives us the victory through our Lord Jesus Christ.
58 Therefore, my beloved brethren, be you steadfast, unmoveable, always abounding in the work of the Lord, forasmuch as you know that your labour is not in vain in the Lord.

What a glorious thing God has in store for us. That our bodies will not inherit the kingdom of God. Because our bodies have ailments, injuries, and other sadness. Paul speaks of this change earlier as being like a seed planted. The dead body of the seed is changed into a new and living thing. This change that is to be is one of corruption and one of immortality. We will be free from the temptation to sin. Death will have lost its sting! There will be no grave to swallow us up. Instead, the victory we have belongs to the Lord!

Dear Lord Jesus,

Empower me to share this promise with my fellow believers, and to plant seeds where You will water so that they too may find a love of You who give us so much. Lord, use me, that I may share my reasons for joy in Your overpowering love.

In Jesus name, Amen.

Day #70
I Corinthians 16:1-4

1   Now concerning the collection for the saints, as I have given order to the churches of Galatia, even so do you.
2   Upon the first *day* of the week let every one of you lay by him in store, as *God* hath prospered him, that there be no gatherings when I come.
3   And when I come, whomsoever you shall approve by *your* letters, them will I send to bring your liberality unto Jerusalem.
4   And if it be meet that I go also, they shall go with me.

Paul speaks to the gatherings in Corinth as having received the same directions as all of Galatia. That when he comes to preach on the first day of the week then day comes, that there need be no offerings/collections. The store he referred to is how people saved their offerings. They put it in store, so as to give to others and the church. He does speak of delivering the offering to the saints in Jerusalem; a mission's collection that the church in Corinth was engaging in.

Dear Lord Jesus,

May You be blessed by what we lay in store and with what we give. Lord, direct our steps in putting things aside so that Your love may be shared around the world. Lord, encourage me to think more of those who need help so that I may lay more in store to give to support that work.

In Jesus name, Amen.

Day #71
I Corinthians 16:5-9

5   Now I will come unto you, when I shall pass through Macedonia: for I do pass through Macedonia.
6   And it may be that I will abide, yea, and winter with you, that you may bring me on my journey whithersoever I go.
7   For I will not see you now by the way; but I trust to tarry a while with you, if the Lord permit.
8   But I will tarry at Ephesus until Pentecost.
9   For a great door and effectual is opened unto me, and *there are* many adversaries.

In this closing of his letter to the Corinthians, Paul tells them of his intention to return to them. He gives them a time period for his plans to be there, but his plans are dependent on God's will. It is good to make plans and have plans, but we need to accept that God may have different plans and to put His direction first. First and foremost, Paul is going where God leads him. This great door the Lord opened that Paul should minister in, Paul cannot turn down, even though he knows there are dangers involved in ministering there. He still must do as God leads.

Dear Lord Jesus,

I know you direct my path. Lord, help me to see Your will as I begin to make plans. Lord, enable to me see some of Your plans for me so that I may become more of what You desire and become prepared for the things You desire to use me for.

In Jesus name, Amen.

Day #72
I Corinthians 16:10-24

10   Now if Timotheus come, see that he may be with you without fear: for he worketh the work of the Lord, as I also *do*.

11   Let no man therefore despise him: but conduct him forth in peace, that he may come unto me: for I look for him with the brethren.

12   As touching *our* brother Apollos, I greatly desired him to come unto you with the brethren: but his will was not at all to come at this time; but he will come when he shall have convenient time.

13   Watch you, stand fast in the faith, quit you like men, be strong.

14   Let all your things be done with charity.

15   I beseech you, brethren, (you know the house of Stephanas, that it is the firstfruits of Achaia, and *that* they have addicted themselves to the ministry of the saints,)

16	That you submit yourselves unto such, and to every one that helps with *us*, and labours.
17	I am glad of the coming of Stephanas and Fortunatus and Achaicus: for that which was lacking on your part they have supplied.
18	For they have refreshed my spirit and yours: therefore acknowledge you them that are such.
19	The churches of Asia salute you. Aquila and Priscilla salute you much in the Lord, with the church that is in their house.
20	All the brethren greet you. Greet you one another with an holy kiss.
21	The salutation of *me*, Paul with mine own hand.
22	If any man love not the Lord Jesus Christ, let him be Anathema Maranatha.
23	The grace of our Lord Jesus Christ *be* with you.
24	My love *be* with you all in Christ Jesus. Amen.

Paul mentions Timothy who he has sent, that they should accept him and not despise him. He does not share here of his young age. Instead, Paul lifts him up as a fellow laborer for Christ.

Paul lifts up Apollos next as a friend and fellow laborer for Christ. This makes the divisions of the church spoken of earlier nothing but foolishness. Paul and Apollos were friends, so much so that Paul asked Apollos to come to them.

Paul continues by asking them to "standfast in the faith," to be strong, and watchful. We all need to delve into the Word of God to fill this obligation and we need time in prayer, so we can grow in Christ.

Paul next mentions and lifts up fellow laborers in Corinth and asks that the church submit to their work of love for Christ.

In closing of this letter, Paul sends his love. Not as a man, but as a father's love of those who are his spiritual children. A father's love is always.

Dear Lord Jesus,

Thank You for this time in Your Word, learning about Paul's first letter to the Corinthians. Lord, I ask that You continue to keep me growing in You through the reading of Your Word. It is continuing to work on me and make me into a better person.

In Jesus name, Amen.